DIVERSITY INTELLIGENCE

HOW TO CREATE A CULTURE OF INCLUSION FOR YOUR BUSINESS

HEIDI R. ANDERSEN

WILEY

This edition first published 2021
© 2021 Heidi R. Andersen

Registered office
John Wiley & Sons Ltd, The Atrium, Southern Gate, Chichester, West Sussex, PO19 8SQ,
United Kingdom

This work was produced in collaboration with Write Business Results Limited.
For more information on Write Business Results' business book, blog, and podcast
services, please visit their website: www.writebusinessresults.com, email us on
info@ writebusinessresults.com or call us on 020 3752 7057.

For details of our global editorial offices, for customer services and for information about how to
apply for permission to reuse the copyright material in this book please see our website at www.
wiley.com.

Wiley publishes in a variety of print and electronic formats and by print-on-demand. Some material
included with standard print versions of this book may not be included in e-books or in print-on-
demand. If this book refers to media such as a CD or DVD that is not included in the version you
purchased, you may download this material at http://booksupport.wiley.com. For more information
about Wiley products, visit www.wiley.com.

Designations used by companies to distinguish their products are often claimed as trademarks. All
brand names and product names used in this book are trade names, service marks, trademarks
or registered trademarks of their respective owners. The publisher is not associated with any
product or vendor mentioned in this book.

Limit of Liability/Disclaimer of Warranty: While the publisher and author have used their best
efforts in preparing this book, they make no representations or warranties with respect to the
accuracy or completeness of the contents of this book and specifically disclaim any implied
warranties of merchantability or fitness for a particular purpose. It is sold on the understanding
that the publisher is not engaged in rendering professional services and neither the publisher
nor the author shall be liable for damages arising herefrom. If professional advice or other expert
assistance is required, the services of a competent professional should be sought.

Library of Congress Cataloging-in-Publication Data is Available:

ISBN 9781119798880 (hardback)
ISBN 9781119798903 (ePDF)
ISBN 9781119798897 (ePub)

Cover Design: Wiley
Cover Image: © aluxum/E+/Getty Images

SKY83ABFF69-E7A9-4CBA-9526-23888DCDE450_083121

To Jens, my life companion and guardian angel.

CONTENTS

FOREWORD

I am a white, heterosexual, cisgender male. My diversity footprint is not just small, it is virtually non-existent. I could hardly be more privileged. Even if I tried not to be, a patriarchal and racist system would reward me anyway, simply for being who and what I am.

Acknowledging and understanding my privilege, dealing with its consequences, and deconstructing its negative effects on different social groups has been a big challenge for me. Yet, that is nothing compared to the challenges of the non-privileged or marginalized who must face and deal with systemic discrimination every day.

The debate around white male privilege and my own challenge to grapple with it are key to understanding and changing the paradigms of exclusive systems and organizations. Only by understanding such systems and their underlying hierarchies can we gradually overcome toxic normativity and lift the burden we force on people who are "different" from our norms.

One of the pivotal moments in patriarchal societies, for instance, is when men become aware of their privilege. Once we are able to acknowledge that we have had a veritable head start simply by identifying as "male" or "white," we slowly begin to grasp and examine the consequences of our privilege. We need to understand how our own socialization within patriarchy has affected our behavior and how that behavior in turn has consequences for us – and the people around us.

The tough thing about privilege is that being privileged does not necessarily feel so great. "Privilege is the absence of inconvenience, an impediment, or challenge. When you have it, you don't really notice it, but when it's absent, it affects everything you do."[1]

What psychologist and former NBA player John Aemichi says is the very reason privilege, and especially the unawareness of it, stands in the way of truly creating inclusive systems: systems in which each and every one of us can unfold their full potential without having to deny certain aspects of their personality or character. Such systems, however, do not yet exist.

Instead, we foster normative societies and organizations in which only certain social groups feel like they belong while others are left out. And even worse: The cognitive load of constantly having to adapt to circumstances that do not meet one's own needs is one of the major obstacles for belonging. It drains a lot of energy from people from the out-group. The playing field is not level, so one group always has to work harder than the other.

Many privileged people, however, do not feel the need to create more inclusive systems. That does not necessarily make them bad people. They just do not realize that the core of privilege is that a problem isn't perceived as a problem because it isn't *your* problem. Many people do not understand the role they play in the harmful practice of marginalization and discrimination. Instead, they believe that they are about to lose something: For someone who is accustomed to privilege, equality feels like oppression.

The absence of privilege, on the other hand, leads to systemic imbalances regarding access for people who are not part of the privileged in-group. Therefore, we need to understand people's access to our systems. What does the world look like for someone who is non-white, trans,

---

[1] https://www.youtube.com/watch?v=vbPJfxRYmCg.

homosexual, poor, disabled, illiterate, introvert and/or else? How does our world feel for others, for people who are different from us?

"People who are different from us" is a quite accurate definition of the concept of diversity, which goes way beyond the binary and narrow debate of male vs. female. We are so much more than just men and women, black or white, disabled or able-bodied. We are complex human beings, living together in complex social systems. Thus, a debate about how we want to live and work together without understanding the concept of intersectionality is impossible.

Kimberlé Crenshaw, Distinguished Professor of Law at the UCLA School of Law, who introduced and developed the concept of intersectionality, describes its impact as follows: "It's basically a lens, a prism, for seeing the way in which various forms of inequality often operate together and exacerbate each other. We tend to talk about race inequality as separate from inequality based on gender, class, sexuality, or immigrant status. What's often missing is how some people are subject to all of these, and the experience is not just the sum of its parts."[2]

Before we can embark on a journey towards inclusion, we need to acknowledge the systemic experiences of different social groups as well as the interdependency of their social features. We need to understand how intersectional setups define whether a human being has access to our systems – or not. And the key to understanding that difference in access is empathy.

Diversity is a fact; inclusion is the path; belonging is the goal. For many people, this is already a paradigm shift. They still believe in some kind of "diversity endgame." That explains why so many organizations are currently jumping on the bandwagon by bragging about their diversity initiatives. But

---

[2] https://time.com/5786710/kimberle-crenshaw-intersectionality/.

what they are actually doing has little to do with a fundamental change of systemic frameworks. Instead, they are feeding their own culture gaps.

Organizations can be privileged, too. It's the *privilege of interpretation* many companies claim for themselves. They interpret their own approaches towards being fair and inclusive far too optimistically. One might call that practice "pinkwashing," adding to what organizational change theorists call the culture gap: the gap between the *culture as intended (CAI)* and the *culture as practiced (CAP)*. This gap between talking and doing can become very dangerous for an organization. Once the gap becomes too big, companies can implode.

Many companies still believe in the "tale of the pipeline." They think that just by adding women or PoC to their pipeline, the whole system will change. But representation does not automatically lead to participation. Quite the opposite is the case, actually. If all we do is add people from the diversity drawing board, we are throwing these people under the bus. Organizational cultures often work like an immune system: They attack every outsider who does not belong.

Inclusion is hard work, especially because diversity itself can be very demanding, exhausting even. Not only do we have to overcome our biased assessment of people and circumstances, we also need to find intrinsic motivation while doing so. Extrinsic metrics alone, however, are not enough to change the practice of unconsciously installing and upholding exclusive, in-group oriented monocultures.

At some point, we need to believe in what we are doing. Apart from financial or political aspects, we need to embrace the idea that it is the right thing to do to create systems based on equal opportunities. Our KPIs should not be awards or manifestos or quantitative metrics from the pipeline only – but a feeling of belonging for those who have not yet had equal access.

Our approach to understanding these facts and putting the necessary steps in motion must be an empathic one, not just a rational one. We need to educate ourselves and learn about our conceptual biases, such as intersectionality and privilege. DEB (diversity, equity, belonging) is nothing less than empathy training. It can be very challenging. It also needs a humble perspective by those who are already part of the in-group. But the result is worth every effort.

The key to change is a process of reflection for men, because men are holding positions of power. And with power, there comes responsibility. We need to become aware of our privilege, especially if we do not feel or experience it. If we feel accused, neglected, or blamed by all those attempts to heal a sexist, misogynist, exclusive, classist monocultural system, then we still have a lot of work to do.

We are key players in that process. We need to become allies in changing the system. We need to live up to our responsibilities and play a role as agents of change. We need to identify how, when, and where our behavior harms people who are different from us. Then, and only then, can we enable our organizations and our systems to become truly inclusive.

Robert Franken is a German consultant, speaker, and activist. He advises organizations and top executives on the subjects of transformation, DIB, and organizational change. Now an expert for organizational culture, Franken used to be the CEO of various tech and community startups. He is on the advisory board of PANDA, a German network for female executives. In 2016, he founded the platform "Male Feminists Europe." He is one of six honorary catalysts for HeForShe Germany.

ACKNOWLEDGEMENTS

So many people have knowingly and unknowingly inspired me to write this book:

All the passionate people in businesses around the world who believe in transforming their companies and unleashing the potential of diversity and who trusted in us and reached out to embark on the journey together.

My colleagues Kasper Jelsbech Knudsen and Salman S. Ahmad, who are experts in this field and know how to apply their knowledge and wisdom to create actual improvements.

My soul sister Helle Katholm Knutsen, an ever inexhaustible source of inspiration, of uncontrollable mind journeys and transformative conversations, some of which are scattered in this book.

Jens Rottbøll for encouraging me to take the time, we both knew I did not have, and for patiently believing and investing in this project.

My grandsons Birk, Frej and Eik for unconsciously energising me when I most needed it.

Georgia Kirke and Katherine Lewis from Write Business Results who skillfully stood by my side through the writing process.

INTRODUCTION

I would like to start by telling you why I am writing this book. Diversity and Inclusion (D&I) is an area that I am incredibly passionate about. Through this book, I want to help more companies enhance their ability to stay in the market by implementing D&I initiatives that work. I want to improve wellbeing and psychological safety in workplaces and I want companies to become more innovative by attracting and retaining talent, no matter what that talent looks like, and to benefit financially from it.

Most of all, I want this book to help many more companies harness the many benefits of diversity and inclusion. As we at the Living Institute have discovered, the best way to do this is by developing what we call *diversity intelligence*. In this book, I will share why diversity intelligence can foster an inclusive culture in your organisation, one that attracts, motivates, engages and retains the most talented people you can possibly find. You will learn all the key steps to take (and those to avoid) and I will also share how to get others on board to create the necessary mindset shift, but first, let me take you back to the time when I first realised how diversity affected me.

Cake, liquorice and an unfortunate Danish company

I have been living and working in a diverse setting my whole life. Even as a child, I realised that a person's cultural background has a big impact on norms, values and behaviours.

My mother is a Danish Lutheran and my father is a Catholic from Southern Germany, so I grew up with a dual cultural background. There was a big difference between my grandparents' home in Denmark and my grandparents' home in Germany.

Very quickly, I realised that I had to change my behaviour to earn their affection. I adapted my behaviour in Southern Germany to get as much cake as possible and I adapted my behaviour in Denmark to get as much liquorice as possible.

Basically, there were two versions of me, and by understanding and navigating the different cultural norms between my grandparents, I profited from them as a child.

What I noticed as I grew up and joined the workforce was that many large global companies were struggling with managing and bridging cultural differences within the workplace. My experience at one global company particularly stands out in my memory. My new job was at this company's headquarters. I left my previous job in an organisation characterised by a high degree of diversity, and my family and I left the capital where we lived and moved to the other end of the country. Immediately, we noticed people's reactions to us "big-city" people. We were the odd ones out. Having been used to the multi-cultural and diverse environment in the city, arriving at a company whose staff and culture I would characterise as homogenous was a struggle for me and, in particular, my children. However, we were not the only ones who struggled to fit in.

At that time, the company had relocated an Italian executive from one of its subsidiaries to the headquarters due to his remarkable results in Italy. Back then, he was one of the only non-Danes at the headquarters. However, I immediately saw the resistance he met simply because he was so culturally different. His outgoing way of approaching people was in stark contrast to the culture in the community, both within and outside of the company. I noticed this so clearly because I too felt this resistance. Needless to say, within a short while he left to work for another global company, and so did I. The lack of inclusion at this Danish company, primarily due to a culture of sameness or homogeneity, meant that it became difficult to retain talented staff who did not fit the mould. The company was missing out.

What I realised through this experience is that once you have worked in a highly culturally diverse and inclusive setting, you cannot go back.

It's nothing personal – it's systemic

One of the challenges with bringing the conversation surrounding diversity and inclusivity to the fore is that it can lead to a blame game. Many men, in particular, can feel as though they are being blamed, even though they have not consciously contributed to the current situation.

On many occasions, I have heard middle-aged white men say, "I'm not part of the diversity ambition. I am the one whose fault it is and now I have to lose everything." This could not be further from the truth. In fact, in my experience, many men in this position want to change and make a difference; however, they do not want to be blamed in the process. Blame is not part of the diversity intelligence conversation. My aim is to support these men and encourage them to be actively involved in cultural transformations, because it is when you can mobilise these men that you start to see real progress. Attracting and retaining the best people is only one piece of the puzzle; it is by no means the only reason why organisations should care about inclusion. Another important aspect is sustainable governance, which is underpinned by diversity intelligence.

Enhancing diversity intelligence is sustainable governance

In business, when you talk about sustainability it always comes down to three areas: environmental, social and governance (ESG). Diversity intelligence is an essential element of sustainable governance.

More and more companies are being measured on how they are performing in relation to ESG and sustainability, which is why inclusion of diversity is becoming an increasingly pressing issue for many businesses.

Overview of the book

In the first part of this book, we take a closer look at what diversity intelligence is and how it can be applied within organisations. Chapter 2 takes a deep dive into the business case for diversity intelligence, highlighting the strong financial incentives for choosing the right initiatives that will create a culture of inclusion. We close this part of the book by examining why more progress has not already been made in this area.

Once we understand that background for diversity intelligence, we can look at how to move forward and create more inclusive businesses. Parts 2 and 3 are full of practical advice for creating the necessary cultural transformation where diversity intelligence goes far beyond the surface of an organisation.

I share best practice examples that have been gathered through the work of the Living Institute and our 17 years of experience helping companies in the field of inclusion and diversity.

Among the topics I cover are the roles and responsibilities that allow diversity intelligence to succeed, including why synchronising top management is such an essential part of the process. I share a simple tool to ensure your diversity intelligence strategy is focusing on the right initiatives, helping you to avoid the most common pitfalls that many businesses land in over and over again.

I also talk about unconscious bias, cultural intelligence and gender balance, all of which are huge topics on their own. Understanding these areas and how to navigate them plays a vital role in building a diverse and inclusive company.

The final part of the book returns to some of the most important concepts and paints a picture of the future we are moving towards. Diversity and inclusion is no longer a "nice to have" – it is an essential building block for adaptable and resilient businesses that can navigate an increasingly uncertain world.

Are you ready for change?

If you are reading this book it is likely that you already understand the need for cultural transformation surrounding D&I within your organisation. Maybe you have attempted to introduce D&I initiatives in the past and have seen them fail. Maybe you can see your competitors harnessing diversity and pulling ahead. Maybe you are new to this concept and want to make sure you get your D&I strategy right the first time.

As Founding Partner and Head of Training at the Living Institute, I have encountered businesses in all of these situations and many more. We work with large, global organisations where people often feel as though they are treading water with their D&I strategies or, even worse, slowly sinking. Trust me when I tell you that there is a path towards a brighter future, and I hope to guide your way towards it through this book.

Whatever the practicalities of your specific situation, the reason you are here is the same: you are ready for a change.

There are compelling arguments for enhancing diversity, but, as you will soon learn, the real key to lasting cultural transformation is inclusion by applying diversity intelligence.

James Baldwin, the American essayist, writing passionately about racial discrimination, said: "Not everything that is faced can be changed, but nothing can be changed until it is faced."[1]

Let's get started.

---

[1] James Baldwin in the manuscript to his unfinished *Remember This House*.

Part 1

Introducing Diversity Intelligence

Definition: Diversity Intelligence means the way in which any human system is designed to attract, motivate, engage and retain people with diverse profiles who, through shared inclusion, can leverage their diversity to create better results.

This book is centred around the concept of diversity intelligence as defined above. But why introduce diversity intelligence as a concept now? Well, there is one main reason for this: a new conversation around diversity spurred on by the Black Lives Matter and #MeToo movements that both target a systemic change. To see this more clearly, let us briefly take a look at the concept of diversity in its historical contexts.

Origins of diversity

As a concept, diversity developed under different societal and historical contexts, primarily in the US and Europe. In the US, diversity is often traced back to the Civil Rights Act signed in 1964, whereby it became illegal for employers to discriminate against workers – future or existing – based on identity markers such as race and ethnicity, their gender, nationality or religious background. Much later, in 2008, the topic of diversity was renewed by focusing on the emerging tech industry in Silicon Valley and their diversity statistics, i.e. the representation of women and people of colour in various parts of these organisations.

The (disappointing) results from these transparent investigations, as first reported by San Jose's *Mercury News*,[1] helped to spark stakeholder pressure for these tech companies to continuously show their diversity numbers and document efforts to improve them – beginning, perhaps most famously, with Google publishing their diversity report in 2014.

Meanwhile, in Europe, conversations about diversity centred around the issue of equality and, more specifically, gender equality and the integration, or in some cases assimilation, of people from different ethnic and cultural backgrounds. Many were from former European colonies, while others were labour migrants or refugees from war-torn parts of the world.[2]

The point here is that in the European and US historical contexts, the concept of diversity developed mainly because of an inability to integrate diversity into these societies in a meaningful and inclusive way to begin with. This brings us to the need for systemic change, which is what diversity intelligence targets.

---

[1]Swift, M. (2010), "Five Silicon Valley Companies Fought Release of Employment Data, and Won", *The Mercury News*, 11 February 2010, available at: https://www.mercurynews.com/2010/02/11/five-silicon-valley-companies-fought-release-of-employment-data-and-won/.

[2]Laufer, J. (2009), "Is Diversity the Answer to Gender Equality?", *Travail, Genre et Sociétés*, Volume 21 (Issue 1): 29–54, available at: https://www.cairn-int.info/article-E_TGS_021_0029–is-diversity-the-answer-to-gender-equali.htm.

Recently, global movements such as Black Lives Matter and #MeToo have irreversibly challenged our blindness to systemic prejudices and the power of privilege. It is no longer possible to talk only about individual behaviour, the few rotten apples. What is needed is a much broader and more holistic approach that aims to change cultural systems. People interact within more or less structured systems, be they societies, organisations or schools, for instance, and as such we need to rethink the *design* of our systems to ensure physical and psychological safety, wellbeing and fair opportunities for all.

Diversity intelligence is systemic design

Building upon the insights from Black Lives Matter and #MeToo, we will therefore refer to diversity intelligence as the way to achieve inclusion. As previously mentioned, diversity intelligence means to design a human system to attract, motivate, engage and retain people with diverse profiles who, through shared inclusion, can leverage their diversity to create better results.

Diversity intelligence will allow us to build up our capacity and courage to open our minds and hearts, and strengthen relations to those who are not like us. In other words, we need diversity intelligence to ensure that we can achieve a balanced representation of people who reflect the societies and markets in which we operate, to allow us to use the immense power of differences to create the best possible solutions for our own benefit and the benefit of future generations.

Let us say there is an organisation whose competitive advantage is to attract the most talented specialists. As such, the organisation cannot afford to overlook any potential talent due to their gender, age, nationality, skin colour or any other identity marker. Therefore, the organisation decides to redesign every aspect of the employee lifecycle with one goal in mind: the inclusion of all existing and future talent irrespective of their different identities. Not only do they want to design the system to be attractive from the outside, they also want the system to make it easy for talented individuals to be motivated and feel engaged, thereby ensuring that once these talented people are in, they will not want to work anywhere else.

However, what does it mean to design a system with diversity intelligence? Let me use an analogy to simplify this concept.

Diversity intelligence – a walk in the park

Imagine a large city. As in most cities, this one has certain areas that are abandoned by most people and city officials. These are the kind of areas that are left to decay, making them attractive only as informal waste sites and spaces for criminal activity in the lure of darkness at night; the kind of areas that you avoid passing through if you can. They are certainly not places where you want to live.

Now imagine a city council that wants to transform this abandoned and decaying urban space into an attractive park for its citizens while offering housing opportunities to those who might have sought refuge there in the past. To do this, the council first has to get architects and urban landscapers to map out a design based on the existing area where the park will be located. To get the highest possible return on this investment, in a financial and social sense, they want the design to appeal to all the citizens who live in the city. Once the design of the park is in place, construction workers begin clearing the ground and laying new foundations for paths, playgrounds and perhaps even space for open-air exercise equipment and art installations to be placed throughout. Gardeners begin tilling the ground, planting flowers and bushes, and trimming the trees. Perhaps the council decides to also implement accessible transportation to and from the park to make it as easy as possible for everyone to access the renewed space.

Once all these things are in place, it will take little effort to encourage people to use the space as intended. No long "Standard Operating Procedures" are needed to explain the purpose of the park and how it should be used. It is simply built into the environment. Perhaps it is necessary to train people to oversee the park, maintaining it and making sure everyone feels safe, but other than that, you can imagine how quickly the park could be filled with people from all over the city who run and exercise there, who eat their lunch on benches, have picnics on the grass and play with their children. Perhaps even outsiders such as tourists will be attracted to the park to view the art installations or simply escape the crowded streets of the city. This park now has a design that attracts, motivates, engages and retains as many different people as possible. This is what I mean by a diversity intelligent design.

In this book, I am taking you on a walk in this metaphorical park. I will show you how you can design the architecture in your organisation, highlighting what you need to keep in mind to attract, motivate, engage and retain as many people as possible, no matter who they are. I will also show you what you can do to educate those who are responsible for managing this diversity intelligent system and what they need to do to constantly sustain and update it by adjusting to the people within it.

With this definition in mind, diversity intelligence does not have to be an insurmountable task that takes decades to accomplish. In fact, by following the guidelines laid out in this book, implementing a diversity intelligent system is really something of a walk in the park.

Diversity intelligence is the path to inclusion

In the last decade, we have seen a multitude of studies published, many of which you will become familiar with in this book, that show time and again that simply increasing the representation of people from so-called "diverse" backgrounds, meaning, in a somewhat outdated sense, minorities of all kinds, is not enough. In fact, without a *culture of inclusion* these diversity efforts will fail. Inclusion is the end goal, the magic pill for any organisation.

At the Living Institute, we have developed a statistically valid method to measure whether a system is diversity intelligent or not. Our key metric is inclusion. In other words, the purpose of designing a diversity intelligent system is that it results in a shared sense of inclusion. We know from our analysis and surveys measuring the level of inclusion in global companies that, in general, there are two key characteristics of inclusion:

1. Do people feel like they belong within the organisation or their team (i.e. the system)?
2. Do people experience fair and equal career opportunities regardless of the unique and different skills and competencies they contribute?

Combined, people's sense and experiences of belonging and fair opportunities, also referred to as equity, give us an indication of the level of inclusion. As it turns out, the more an organisation implements the guidelines of diversity intelligence as listed in this book, the higher their overall inclusion score. As such, diversity intelligence is the roadmap to inclusion.

Before I take you through the different guidelines for achieving diversity intelligence, let us first examine what it looks like when an organisation is not designed with diversity intelligence in mind. Secondly, we will discover why inclusion and diversity intelligence matter from a business perspective, including why they are increasingly described as business critical.

Chapter 1

A Shift in Mindset

Representation is not a marker of inclusion

At the Living Institute, we encourage all of our clients to view inclusion as the end goal, rather than diversity. This distinction is important, because if you can create a culture of inclusion, you can welcome and include everyone.

Diversity without inclusion is a terrible idea – for the people you hire in and for your company.

People are able to feel whether an environment is inclusive; in fact, most of us have this ability. We might not always be able to point to the specific factors that make a culture or environment feel as though it is inclusive or not, but on a subconscious level we are able to sense whether somewhere, in this case a business, has a high or low degree of inclusion. While research shows us that it does matter that diversity is visible in a company setting, few people who generally are considered to be minority group members prefer to be the token of diversity. Why? Because they want to feel like they are part of the group and be treated the same as everyone else. Just as we all do.

Making diversity work for everyone

We're going to begin by looking back 17 years, to the early days of the Living Institute and a Danish cleaning company we worked with at that time.

When you looked at the lowest levels of that company's hierarchy, there were no Danes working among the cleaning staff. These jobs were held entirely by immigrant workers. However, as soon as you looked even one step higher, all you would see were Danes. The managers in charge of the cleaning teams were Danish, their managers were Danish, and so on all the way to the top.

The Living Institute was invited to deliver a workshop about cultural intelligence to this first tier of managers, because at this time the company was struggling to recruit cleaners of certain nationalities. It transpired that if a manager had a conflict with one person from a particular community, that entire community would refuse to work for this company. Imagine, for example, that a manager had a conflict with a Somali cleaner and, all of a sudden, this company could not recruit any cleaners from the Somali community.

The managers towards the top of the hierarchy were concerned that they might see one community after another blacklisting their company, leaving them with a smaller and smaller pool of people from which to recruit.

When we came in to deliver our workshop, we were tasked with getting the teams of managers further down the hierarchy to see working with non-Danes as a positive.

At the beginning of the workshop, we asked everyone to share their experiences of working with people from all over the world, while we wrote all the statements on a flipchart for everyone to see. Among the stories we heard were that the cleaners went on holiday and never came back, that many prayed most of the time, that some did not respect female superiors, that most of them did not understand work instructions – or they did not *want* to understand instructions, someone said. The them-and-us rhetoric was saturating the room.

We were filling up the flipchart with a long list of complaints. Next, we flipped to a clean sheet of paper and asked the participants what was good about working with non-Danes, and you could hear a pin drop. Finally, someone said, "I really look forward to when the Thai women in my team bring food to work because Thai food tastes so goddamn good." A female participant said, "When I had my first child and came back from maternity leave, some of the women brought me bags full of baby stuff and one had baked a cake to celebrate the event. I was very touched by it."

One person said, "I had the best holiday ever with my family last summer. One of the guys on my team invited us to stay in his family's house in the mountains in Bosnia. It was fabulous, with a swimming pool and all. Our kids loved it. People were warm and welcoming and we became friends with some of his neighbours."

All of a sudden, the room was filled with more and more positive stories, from the Morrocan cleaner who brought a present to someone's house for their son's birthday, to invitations to be the guest of honour at lavish weddings.

As the managers shared more and more examples of positive experiences of working with non-Danes, it became apparent that what made all the difference was not how the non-Danes were different, but rather the feeling of caring for one another and sharing more than their professional roles dictated. What made the difference to these managers were their experiences of being included.

Snapping my fingers

As the talk died down, I addressed this group of 20–25 people and said, "Okay, what if I told you that I had the authority to just snap my fingers and that would mean that when you came into work tomorrow, you'd only be working with Danes, people just like you – would you want me to snap my fingers?"

After an awkward moment, all I heard were statements like, "No, don't do it." I asked, "Why? If I snap my fingers all these problems and complaints you shared on the seven flipcharts earlier would disappear. Everything would be so much easier...."

The responses included, "I actually love the fact that we're not the same" and "I find it very intriguing to learn how they're different from me."

I said, "But is there no turning back? 10 years ago, you were all cleaners in homogenous Danish teams. Don't you want to go back to those days?" The reply was, "No, thinking about it, this is actually so much better."

A them-and-us syndrome had clouded all the positive sides of working with people with a different cultural background to their own. When confronted with the risk of losing the daily encounters with their non-Danish colleagues, it dawned on everyone in the room how much they would lose.

Inclusion is addictive

Even with all the complexities of diversity, the pitfalls and the conflict, we seldom meet anyone who, given the choice, says they wish their organisation would become 100% homogenous again. The thing is you become addicted to inclusion. Without a diversity intelligent mindset, you get stuck in the sameness trap, convincing yourself and others that working with people who are just like you is much better.

"I'm an ethnic minority, female and lesbian. I represent diversity in almost every way. What I need is not to be highlighted as the example of diversity in our company. What I need are fair and equal opportunities and good inclusive leadership."

– Female respondent to an inclusion survey

Why diversity is a sensitive issue

We are moving towards greater diversity more quickly than ever before, but our minds may not always be travelling as fast as reality. In short, some of us are struggling to keep up with the pace of change, from homogeneity as the norm to diversity as the norm, even though when you think of all the invisible diversity parameters, it would be easy to argue that diversity, in some sense, is already the norm.

Diversity is often considered a sensitive topic. There are many reasons for this, but one of the most integral is that many of us are becoming more and more aware of a lack of diversity in many areas and, at the same time, do not know how to change it.

Our communities are becoming much more diverse, so we are seeing greater diversity reflected in the world around us. In addition, there have been several pivotal movements that have catapulted diversity, and particularly inequality, into the global spotlight.

In terms of shining a light on the lack of gender equality within organisations, societies and families, the #MeToo movement has been incredibly powerful. It showed us how big that gender imbalance really is.

Similarly, the Black Lives Matter movement has highlighted the scale of racism within societies around the world. It gained momentum after the unbearable and reprehensible death of George Floyd in the US, and months later it had become a truly global movement. The global attention on diversity and representation has caused societies and organisations to face the reality that many, if not most, social systems are designed to favour and promote those who are already in power. Now, because of these uprisings, we have to ask ourselves: "What are we doing to ensure fair and equal opportunities for all? Have we created a culture where everyone can thrive and contribute with their unique and authentic selves?"

This feeling of not knowing what to do around a lack of diversity is not just a personal problem, it is one that a great number of organisations around the world are grappling with. I would say that the majority of Fortune 500 companies aim to have more females in top management positions, but many simply do not know how to achieve this.

In fact, despite this realisation, in most companies it is a real struggle for women to advance to top-executive level. At the same time, our inclusion surveys and other studies[1] show that women are more ambitious than

---

[1] Abouzahr, K., Krentz, M., Tracey, C., and Tsusaka, M. (2017), *Dispelling the Myths of the Gender "Ambition Gap"*, BCG, 5 April 2017, available at: https://www.bcg.com/publications/2017/people-organization-leadership-change-dispelling-the-myths-of-the-gender-ambition-gap.

men, while companies lose significant sums of money by *not* having women in top management positions.

The issue is incredibly complex, both in terms of the reasons why it is the way it is, and also in terms of why we often cannot make a change even if we want to.

It is a matter of perception

How included we feel in a particular organisation comes down to our own personal identity. We see this all the time when we field inclusion surveys in large companies. There are always groups who feel less included than others, and I hate to say it, but in most organisations it is usually white, middle-aged male respondents who say they feel highly included.

When we compare their answers to the survey to those given by women, women of colour, and women and men with different national or ethnic backgrounds to the majority of those at the headquarters, we generally find significant differences in the levels of inclusion.

Many people in the latter groups do not feel as included and, as a result, they want to leave the company more quickly than those who say they feel very included in the business. Their loyalty is affected simply by virtue of the fact that they do not belong to the majority group.

One study found that the more diversity a company has in its top management, the more loyal millennials are to that business. This is even one of the smoking guns as to why companies with unequal representation and lower levels of diversity lose money compared to their more diverse competitors: because having a higher staff turnover costs money.[2]

---

[2]Deloitte (2018), "Millennial Survey".

Summary

When we stop to think about it and look at the world around us, we can see that diversity, in many cases, is already our norm. However, the key to unlocking the power of diversity within business, as well as broader society, is inclusion.

As Maurice Lévy, chairman of the Publicis Groupe, once said, "When you realise the power of diversity, you keep it as a business secret." We are going to explore the business case for diversity in greater detail now in Chapter 2.

Chapter 2

Where the Money Lies

The dividend of equal representation

In early 2020, Goldman Sachs announced that it would no longer list any companies that did not have at least one diverse board member. This policy applies to all US and European companies and the organisation stated it would continue to increase the number of diverse board members required. Therefore, in 2021, under this policy it will require all companies to have at least two diverse board members in order to be listed with it.

What is interesting is that, in the last two years, Goldman Sachs has listed 60 companies without any female board members, knowing that having at least one diverse board member would result in a 44% increase in a company's average share price within one year of going public. This compares to just a 13% jump in average share price for companies with no diverse board members.

Goldman Sachs listed 60 companies knowing that they would miss out on that significant gain if those companies did not diversify their boards, which, when you think about how much money that actually equates to, is crazy.

What's your inclusion score?

In the early spring of 2020, we were contacted by a venture capital fund that had decided it would no longer acquire or invest in companies that were not characterised by a high degree of diversity.

They came to us at the Living Institute to create a way of scoring the diversity of companies and making sure that they had a culture of inclusion. What they wanted was proof that any company they acquired or invested in had a culture of inclusion. They asked us to analyse any companies they were considering for investment or acquisition and give them an inclusion score.

We teamed up with the Technical University of Denmark (DTU Compute) and together we designed a way to measure the level of inclusion in an organisation. This is essentially a gap analysis that is designed to assess a company's ability to master diversity.

In addition to analysing the culture of inclusion at each company, the venture capital fund also wanted us to provide a report setting out what the company would need to do in order to reach a high inclusion score.

This would include our diagnosis of the areas that were not working, such as the leaders not being equipped with the right tools, recruitment processes excluding talent, the level of unconscious bias within an organisation and women not feeling valued or as though they belonged in a company. Our report also provided a roadmap for these companies, showing them what initiatives they needed to put in place to close these gaps.

If, after a period of time, we could see that these companies were taking the "medicine" we had prescribed for them and were closing the perception gaps within their organisation, the venture capital fund would then invest in them.

This is something we hear from more and more venture and equity funds: they no longer invest in companies that do not have inclusion as part of their DNA.

The dividend of enhanced gender balance

As I mentioned towards the end of Chapter 1, gender balance has also been found to have a significant positive impact on the financial performance of businesses, and it's getting noticed.

"From a governance perspective, diversity on boards is a very very important issue," CEO of Goldman Sachs, David Solomon said in 2020, and announced that the investment bank would no longer list companies that did not have women represented in top management. Now, I do not think they made that decision because they are particularly fond of women; they made it because they are experts on financial growth. "Starting on July 1st in the U.S. and Europe, we're not going to take a company public unless there's at least one diverse board candidate, with a focus on women," Solomon said on CNBC's "Squawk Box" from the World Economic Forum in Davos, Switzerland. "And we're going to move towards 2021 requesting two," he added.

"About 60 companies in the U.S. and Europe have gone public recently with all white, male boards," he said.

"Look, we might miss some business, but in the long run, this I think is the best advice for companies that want to drive premium returns for their shareholders over time," Solomon concluded.[1]

At the beginning of 2020, Goldman Sachs released figures that showed having women in top management positions enabled companies to outperform their competitors and improve their bottom lines by 2.5%. That is

---

[1]Squawk Box (2020), "Goldman CEO says firm won't take companies public that don't have at least one diverse board member", *CNBC* 23 January 2020, available at: https://www.cnbc.com/video/2020/01/23/goldman-sachs-ceo-ipo-diversity-squawk-box-interview.html.

a lot of money and it demonstrates that it is not only the share price that increases, but also the annual return of the business.

A study[2] from 2017 of 11,000 publicly traded companies worldwide conducted by another banker, Robert Næss, Portfolio Manager and Chief Investment Officer in the Scandinavian bank Nordea, found that a company with a female CEO or head of the board had a 25% annualised return since 2009, which is more than double the 11% delivered by the MSCI World Index.

"If you invested in a company with a woman at the helm, you would have outperformed the market," said Robert Næss.

Despite this, only 4% of the top 500 biggest companies in the world have women at the helm at the time of writing.

Why is gender balance important in business?

We are not going to look at the money perspective in detail here, but it is always valid to ask, "Why do the companies with gender balance (or some gender balance) outperform the companies without it?"

Research from McKinsey talks about the difference in leadership characteristics between men and women, but one of the key things to recognise is that companies these days are much more complex than they were 20 or 30 years ago. You need diversity of thought and diversity of leadership skills to cope with the complexity that modern companies face.[3]

---

[2]Nordea (2017), "Investing in female CEOs pays off", 9 August 2017, available at: https://www.nordea.com/en/press-and-news/news-and-press-releases/news-en/2017/investing-in-female-ceos-pays-off.html.
[3]McKinsey (2008), "Women Matter 2: Female Leadership, a competitive edge for the future".

What we are talking about here is the staying power of companies. You have to ask whether your company will be gone five years from now if you do not know how to respond to that complexity and navigate it. What we have observed is that, when men and women are working and leading together, a company's ability to navigate that complexity improves.

Through this approach, you are moving away from the sameness of thinking to diversity of thought by virtue of the simple fact that men and women lead differently and, when their approaches are combined, create better results.

One difference that you can measure is that women tend to ask more questions than men. Women are more likely to speak up and say, "Is what we're doing now a good idea?" For example, I cannot imagine that there was a female engineer in the room when Volkswagen decided to make their emissions-cheating devices. If a woman had been present, she would have been much more likely to ask that all-important question: "What if they find out?" When that scandal broke, Volkswagen lost $16.9 billion of its market value in a matter of days, and they had to set aside $18 billion to cover the cost of fines, legal claims and recalls related to diesel emissions-cheating in the United States and other countries. Would they have taken that path and lost that money if someone had questioned that course of action? Boris Groysberg and Deborah Bell offer several interesting perspectives. One of them is that many female directors noted that they were more likely than their male counterparts to ask tough questions or move boardroom discussions forward in skilled and effective ways.[4]

Perhaps there were women in the room, and perhaps they did not ask that billion dollar question. If so, there might be an explanation as to why they did not ask the question, and that explanation might be a concept called covering; but let's not get ahead of ourselves.

---

[4]Bell, D. and Groysberg, B. (2013), "Dysfunction in the Boardroom", *Harvard Business Review*, June 2013.

Research shows us that, when women are on boards, male CEOs are less overconfident.[5] We can also see evidence that companies with women in top management positions tend to be more risk averse and sustainable, all because women simply have a tendency to ask these "What if?" questions.

This highlights the importance of having a mix of both genders in top management positions. I want to stress here that it is having the balance between men and women that makes all the difference. This is not about replacing all the men in management positions with women, far from it.

Historically, the world has catered more for men than it has for women and there is a misconception among some people that, in order for women to move into these positions of power, decision-making and authority, men have to lose. What I and the rest of the Living Institute focus on is diversity from a place of inclusivity. Diversity works best when *all* the different identity groups come together, not when one is prioritised over another. However, we must acknowledge that equality may feel like discrimination if you belong to the privileged groups.

Even five years ago, I would have thought it was a bad idea to hire one woman to an executive team consisting of men, because I would have been concerned that she would feel like the odd one out, that she could not be authentic and therefore might hide sides of herself to fit in (this is the concept of *covering*, which we will explore in greater detail in Chapter 9).

What is apparent in countries such as Norway and France, that have introduced legislation stipulating that 40% of boards need to be made up

---

[5]Chen, J., Goergen, M., Leung, W.S., and Song, W. (2019), "Research: When Women Are on Boards, Male CEOs Are Less Overconfident", *Harvard Business Review*, 12 September 2019, available at: https://hbr.org/2019/09/research-when-women-are-on-boards-male-ceos-are-less-overconfident.

of women, is that even though these women were, in part, chosen for their roles based on their gender, they still had a positive effect on the bottom line result.

The link between innovation and diversity

A study by the Technical University of Munich and Boston Consulting Group[6] in 2017 showed how much more innovative companies are when there is equal representation and a high degree of diversity within the organisation, and particularly in top management.

There are certain diversity parameters that seem to have an especially profound impact. The parameters identified in this study that made the biggest difference to innovation were gender and cultural diversity.

Gender balance was highlighted as particularly important. The study found that, if you have one woman out of 10 people, you see a certain positive effect. That positive effect increases if you have two women out of 10 people. However, once you reach a figure of three women out of 10, you see exponential growth in innovation power.

To me, the bottom line is, therefore, why just hire one woman when you could hire three? Let us imagine that if you just have one woman on a board with nine men, there is a risk she might not raise her voice and ask the kinds of questions we talked about earlier. However, if there are three women, there is a much greater chance that one of them will raise her voice to ask those important questions, which is why we see a greater positive effect when more than just one woman is introduced to a board.

---

[6]Brosi, P., Lorenzo, R., Schetelig, K., Voigt, N., Welpe, I., and Zawadzki, A. (2017), "The Mix That Matters", Boston Consulting Group and Technical University of Munich, 26 April 2017, available at: https://www.bcg.com/en-gb/publications/2017/people-organization-leadership-talent-innovation-through-diversity-mix-that-matters.

What sparks the discussion about gender balance on boards?

Whenever a company calls us to ask for our help with improving gender balance at the higher levels, we always ask why they are calling *now*. What prompted them to pick up the phone and get in touch? Nine times out of ten, it is because a board member has told the CEO that they want to see more diversity and better gender balance in top management.

When we ask why, specifically, they want to have more women in top-level positions, they usually say it is to enable them to look after shareholders' interests and to make sure they get as much money as possible from the company.

Some companies attach targets to it, such as wanting a 50/50 gender balance at all levels by 2025 or 2030. Really, the point is that board members are telling their CEOs that they need to make this happen. They are telling them that now is the time to fast-forward this agenda.

Money talks. . .

As we saw from the figures published by Goldman Sachs, having women in top management positions can have a significant impact on both the bottom line and share price of a business. However, this is not just about gender balance. Improved diversity in a broader sense in management teams also has a positive impact.

A study published by Credit Suisse in 2019 found that companies with more diverse management teams outperformed their competitors with below average diversity in their top management by almost 4% per year.[7]

---

[7]Credit Suisse Research Institute (2019), "The Changing Face of Companies".

This shows that, while having a female executive can improve business performance, having diversity in the broader sense has an even bigger impact.

Doing the math

I recently delivered a talk to members of the Danish government, as well as a number of dignitaries, and, as part of my presentation, I did the math across five of the 20 largest companies in Denmark. I picked the companies at random, but they all had 100% homogenous executive teams.

I only worked out how much more they would have made based on the 2.5% figure than that of Deloitte, to be conservative, but even based on that increase alone, Denmark's GDP would grow by billions every year if companies had more diverse executive teams. It is what I call free money, because you do not have to open a new factory or merge with another company to access it. All you have to do is not reproduce the past.

I would urge you now to look at the top management in your organisation. If it is 100% homogenous, look at the bottom line result in your most recent annual report. If you put a woman in that top team, you can add at least 2.5% to that. If you introduce a woman and somebody with a different cultural background to your top team, you can add 4% to that figure. If you replace a male CEO with a female CEO or chair of the board, you can double the annual return. Doesn't that sound appealing?

Despite the compelling figures and the fact that many companies are thinking about how to introduce more diversity and inclusion into their businesses, very few succeed, and many are failing to act at all.

What is the penalty for failing to act?

Very simply, the penalty for failing to act on diversity and inclusivity initiatives is that the company will most likely be wiped out.

In the short term, you will find that there is a penalty in your bottom line quarterly performance if a lack of diversity persists. A study in 2018 by McKinsey found that, overall, companies in the bottom quartile for both gender and ethnic or cultural diversity were 29% less likely to achieve above average profitability than all the other companies in the dataset.[8]

In short, not only were these companies not leading, they were lagging.

Whenever we start working with a business on improving their gender balance and/or diversity, we always ask, "Is this business critical?" Without hesitation, the answer is always "Yes". There is a broad understanding that, if they don't achieve the gender balance and better representation at the top, that company will fail to exist in even five years' time.

That is what a business-critical issue is: it is one that you have to tackle with urgency, and without taking action you will have no staying power.

Our next questions are, "What part of it is business critical? What makes this business critical?" When we talk to CEOs, their response is often, "We cannot attract and retain the best talent any more."

I recently spoke with an executive of one of the largest companies in Norway about just this issue. The company has been in business for over 120 years and has always attracted the top talent. Now, this executive was saying to me, "The best talent doesn't want to work with us any more. Millennials don't want to work in our company, and the people we can attract aren't competent enough or don't have the potential for developing into great performers."

At the time of writing this book, this company is working with us to make a cultural transformation to ensure it appeals to talent in any shape or form, because its board members are aware that if they do not make a

---

[8]McKinsey (2018), "Delivering through Diversity".

change, they will be unable to maintain their leading position in the market. It is a business-critical issue.

Two truths: financial benefits and talent acquisition

Clearly, this is a problem that has existed for many years, but what seems to be happening at the moment is that many executives and board members are suddenly becoming aware of the financial impact of doing nothing and of the impact that this has on attracting talent.

It has become a financial truth that if you have diversity in your top management, you will outperform your competitors that do not have diversity in their top management.

It has become a recruitment truth that if you do not have diversity in your top management, you will struggle to attract the best talent in your industry.

These two truths are not up for discussion any more. Executives and board members carry these truths with them. The discussions all centre around how can we introduce more diversity into our top management? How can we bring about the necessary cultural change that makes talented individuals choose to work in our organisation?

Although these are the two biggest drivers for change among boards and executives, there are many other benefits to having greater diversity in top management. For example, Juliet Burke released a study in 2018 that found when a business has diversity in its top management, risk is reduced by 30% and innovation is increased by 20%.[9]

---

[9]Australian Institute of Company Directors (2016), "Which Two Heads are Better than One? How diverse teams create breakthrough ideas and make smarter decisions".

I could spend this whole chapter simply sharing all the research coming out of banks, universities, investment funds and so on, but fundamentally everything is pointing in the same direction: diversity and gender balance in top management makes businesses more profitable and more sustainable.

The importance of mastering diversity

In the past, businesses performed perfectly well with 100% homogenous teams. If you go back far enough, there was not even gender balance, let alone any other form of diversity. In this era, you were unlikely to have highly efficient teams, but you were also unlikely to have completely inefficient teams. What you would get was something in the middle: an average.

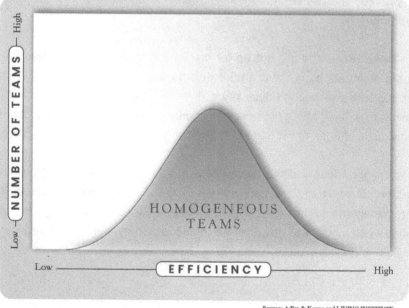

Source: Adler & Kovac and LIVING INSTITUTE

Figure 2.1 Bell curve of observed efficiency in homogenous teams

That meant, for example, if you ran a factory producing bottles of beer, you could confidently say that 100 men could produce 1,000 bottles of beer in a certain period of time – let us say eight hours. If we plot this on a graph, the result is a good old-fashioned bell curve.

Nowadays, it is the opposite. When you have a high number of diverse teams, what you see is that there are far fewer teams with an average output, and more with either incredibly high performance or with incredibly low performance.

You could look at that and wonder why, if I am saying that diversity is such a positive for businesses, there are some diverse teams that perform so poorly. The answer is culture.

OBSERVED EFFICIENCY IN DIVERSE AND HOMOGENOUS TEAMS

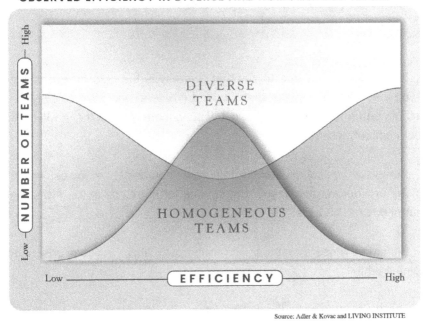

Source: Adler & Kovac and LIVING INSTITUTE

Figure 2.2 Bell curves of observed efficiency in diverse and homog-enous teams

We have to bear in mind that the figures showing that diversity benefits a business's bottom line, like the 4.5% figure calculated by Credit Suisse, take an average across businesses that are considered to be diverse. That means some of those businesses will have highly efficient diverse teams that are probably outperforming their peers by 10–15%, while others with very inefficient diverse teams will be performing worse than their homogenous counterparts.

These inefficient teams drag down the average performance of those companies overall, which is how we arrive at the 4.5% figure.

> *"We have hired some more diverse types – they wear hoodies and sneakers. They challenge things a bit. We can learn from each other and this company can really use their creativity and innovative mindset. But they probably won't stay. This place is too rigid."*
> *– Male respondent to an inclusion survey*

It is therefore not true to say that diversity is the cure for everything. If you are unable to master diversity and create an inclusive culture, it is actually better for you not to have it, because there is a risk that it will make your company less efficient.

However, if you can master diversity at your organisation, you can expect to see an improvement in your bottom line far in excess of the 4.5% estimated by Credit Suisse.

So, what does mastering diversity look like, in comparison to doing it badly?

The bullet points on the left of Figure 2.3 describe a company with a poor working culture. Many of the teams might be diverse, but there

OBSERVED EFFICIENCY IN DIVERSE AND HOMOGENOUS TEAMS

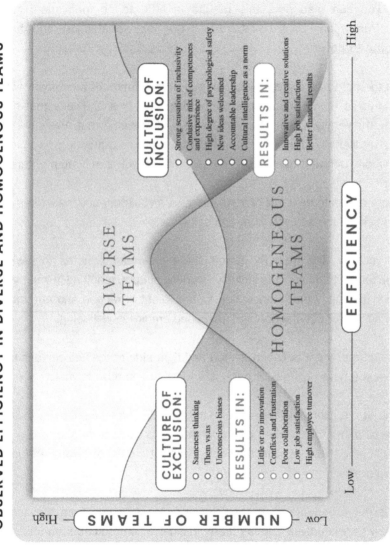

DIVERSE TEAMS

CULTURE OF INCLUSION:
○ Strong sensation of inclusivity
○ Conducive mix of competences and experience
○ High degree of psychological safety
○ New ideas welcomed
○ Accountable leadership
○ Cultural intelligence as a norm

RESULTS IN:
○ Innovative and creative solutions
○ High job satisfaction
○ Better financial results

HOMOGENEOUS TEAMS

CULTURE OF EXCLUSION:
○ Sameness thinking
○ Them vs. us
○ Unconscious biases

RESULTS IN:
○ Little or no innovation
○ Conflicts and frustration
○ Poor collaboration
○ Low job satisfaction
○ High employee turnover

EFFICIENCY

Low — High

NUMBER OF TEAMS

Low — High

Source: Adler & Kovac and LIVING INSTITUTE

Figure 2.3 Bell curves of observed efficiency in diverse and homogenous teams

is a "them-and-us" culture within them and, while some people will feel included, there are others who will feel excluded.

As you can also see, this results in little to no innovation, conflicts, frustration, poor collaboration, low job satisfaction and high employee turnover.

On the right of the graph, you can see a description of a company with many diverse teams that is overperforming. This is a business that has mastered diversity. One of the factors here is ensuring that diversity is a norm. For diversity to flourish, you need to have more than one person in a team who is different to everyone else, and preferably a minimum of three.

There needs to be a mix of competencies and experience, as well as an authenticity in the way you work and collaborate.

As you can see from the graph, there are many benefits to having diverse teams that have this inclusive working culture, resulting in improved decision-making, greater innovation, better talent attraction and retention, higher customer satisfaction and increased employee wellbeing.

The differentiator between the left and right side of the bell curve is not whether you have diversity or not – it is whether you have inclusion or not.

One of the exercises we often do in our inclusion workshops is to ask the participants to rate their own company on a scale from one to five on the bell curve. How well are they doing when it comes to having an inclusive culture?

It is our experience that if all the participants come from the same company they intuitively choose pretty much the same number on the continuum. They see the same patterns and signs of inclusion, or lack of inclusion, manifested in the culture of the company.

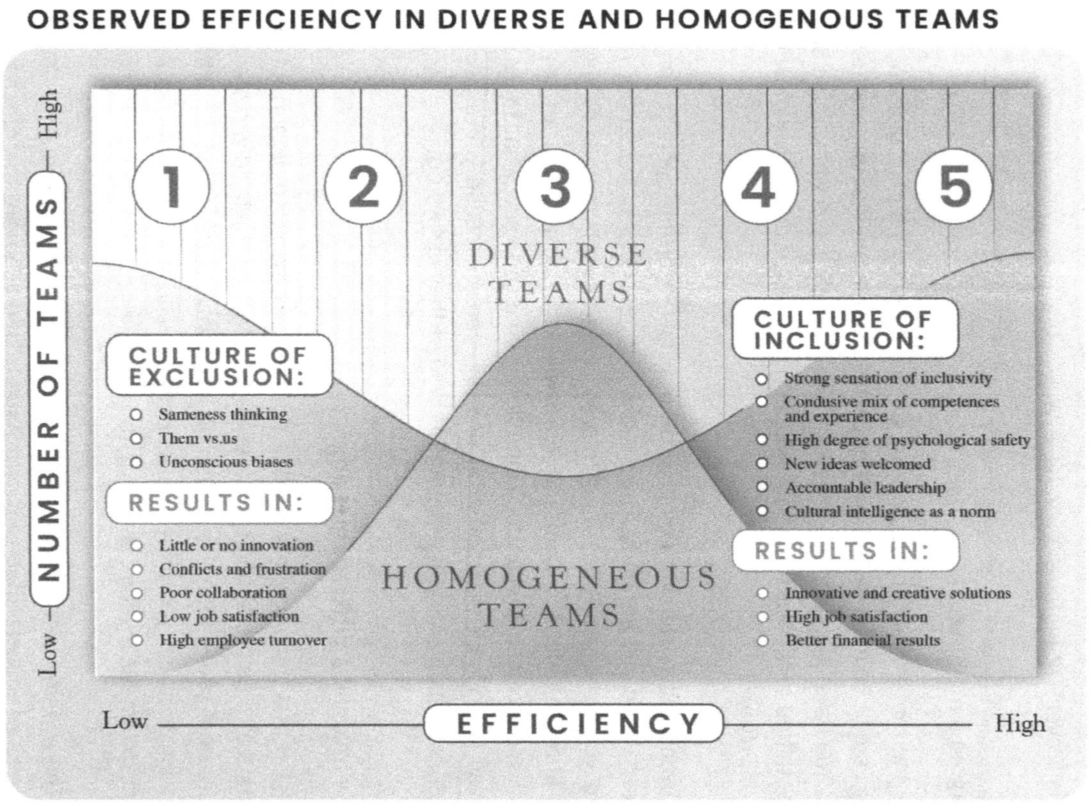

OBSERVED EFFICIENCY IN DIVERSE AND HOMOGENOUS TEAMS

DIVERSE TEAMS

HOMOGENEOUS TEAMS

1   2   3   4   5

CULTURE OF EXCLUSION:
- Sameness thinking
- Them vs.us
- Unconscious biases

RESULTS IN:
- Little or no innovation
- Conflicts and frustration
- Poor collaboration
- Low job satisfaction
- High employee turnover

CULTURE OF INCLUSION:
- Strong sensation of inclusivity
- Condusive mix of competences and experience
- High degree of psychological safety
- New ideas welcomed
- Accountable leadership
- Cultural intelligence as a norm

RESULTS IN:
- Innovative and creative solutions
- High job satisfaction
- Better financial results

NUMBER OF TEAMS — Low / High

EFFICIENCY — Low / High

Source: Adler & Kovac and LIVING INSTITUTE

Figure 2.4   Bell curves of observed efficiency in organisational stages 1 to 5

How diversity benefits decision-making

One of the characteristics of well-functioning diverse teams is that there is an improvement in decision-making. Why is that?

Imagine a meeting. . .

Imagine that tomorrow you have to go to a meeting where important decisions are to be made and the other participants in the meeting are just like you. You have been working together for many years, you went to the same universities and have the same educational backgrounds. You know each other very well.

Even though you are going to be making important decisions in that meeting, and you are going to be making suggestions of how to move forward, you are probably not going to prepare particularly thoroughly because you know that John, Susan and Peter will all agree with you anyway. You have had to make similar decisions before and you knew what to do then, so you go to work that day a bit underprepared because you expect the other participants in that meeting to do what they always do.

Now imagine a different meeting. . .

Imagine that tomorrow you have to go to a meeting where important decisions are to be made and the other participants are highly diverse and different from you in many ways. You do not always agree on all the different perspectives and you know you cannot predict how different people will react to the suggestions you bring to the table.

The evening before that meeting, you prepare very thoroughly. You are going to be making important suggestions and you want the other participants to agree with your perspective. You know, however, that at least three or four of them think differently to you and are likely to come up with other proposals. You want them to choose your suggestion, so you make sure you are well prepared in order to win them over to your point of view.

There is a clear difference in the decision-making process between those two teams. Katherine W. Phillips carried out a study[10] that revealed that these two scenarios I have outlined are what typically happens. The participants in diverse teams are generally much better prepared when they go into meetings and this means their decision-making process is improved. All perspectives are heard and discussed before they finally reach a decision.

According to Cloverpop, a company that provides tools for inclusive decision-making, decision-making drives 95% of business performance. That demonstrates why the way you make decisions matters so much.

Cloverpop[11] studied the DNA of how extremely good business decisions were made. They found that teams with a mix of gender, age and geographic diversity made better decisions 87% of the time, did so twice as fast and with 50% fewer meetings than less diverse teams.

That is where the money lies. Good decision-making is essential to good business performance.

Think back to the Volkswagen example I gave in Chapter 1, where nobody asked that very important question, "What if somebody finds out?" Then think of how much money that decision cost.

---

[10]Phillips, K.W. (2014), "How Diversity Makes Us Smarter", *Scientific American*.
[11]Cloverpop (2017), "Inclusive Decision Making Increases Performance of Diverse Global Companies".

Where to begin with diversity intelligence?

Gender balance is one priority for organisations in terms of improving their inclusivity and diversity. Another area that the world is becoming more and more ready to talk about is that of sexual orientation.

Many people who are heterosexual are increasingly aware that they need to change and challenge the concept that heterosexuality is the norm. As I mentioned earlier, with white, middle-aged men often feeling very included in a workplace and being blind to their privilege of belonging to a majority, the same is true of being heterosexual. Many who identify with this sexual orientation are also blind to their privilege of belonging to a majority.

Being heterosexual and not understanding what it is like to be an LGBTQ person is like being white and not understanding what it is like to be black.

Although gender balance might be the burning issue you are trying to address, it is important not to overlook the positive benefits of improving diversity in other areas. Diversity and inclusion of sexual orientation can be particularly beneficial to organisations in all industries.

Being out at work leads LGBTQ employees to feel safer, more empowered and more creative. A study shows us that those who are open about their sexual orientation at work feel 1.5 times more empowered than their LGBTQ colleagues who have not come out at work. They also feel 1.5 times more able to take creative risks than their LGBTQ colleagues who have not come out.[12]

Let me end this chapter on where the money lies with a quote from Warren Buffett on why he is passionate about gender balance: "Look what's

---

[12]BCG (2020) "A New LGBTQ Workforce Has Arrived – Inclusive Cultures Must Follow".

happened over the past 300 years using half our talent. Just imagine what's gonna happen when we go full blast with 100%."[13]

Summary

There are many benefits to rethinking your organisation in terms of diversity intelligence. You will improve your decision-making processes, you will improve your talent attraction and employee retention, and you will improve your bottom line.

I have outlined the business case in this chapter and I would simply say that if you need a reason to make a change to your company culture, beyond all the benefits it will bring to the individuals who work for you and your teams, do it for the money.

As we have seen, there is a compelling case around the financial truth of having better diversity and inclusion, both at the top levels of your organisation and throughout.

[13]Trevett, I. (2018), "Rich and popular. How does Warren Buffett do it?" *Platinum Business Magazine*, Issue 49 (p. 20), available at: https://education.issuu.com/platinumbusiness/docs/platinum_business_magazine_-_issue__e6cbf0b640d037/20.

Chapter 3

Why Hasn't This Happened Already?

The primary reason why greater progress has not been made in this area is that companies are focusing on diversity but neglecting inclusion.

The point is that you can work as much as you want at bringing more diversity into your company, but if minorities do not feel included, then you will lose them faster than you can hire them. You will also find it difficult to attract them in the first place, because culture is apparent everywhere, from your website to job interviews, and those with the greatest talent, who can pick and choose where they work, will probably take a job with a competitor if they seem more attractive; they just will not take jobs in that kind of environment.

Tackling a toxic culture

The Living Institute conducted an inclusion survey for a large organisation some years ago. As part of the survey, we not only interviewed current employees, but also people who had left the organisation. We wanted to hear their stories about what they had experienced while working there and why they left.

There was one woman's story that particularly stood out and summed up the essence of the culture at this organisation. She had left the organisation six months before we conducted our survey and this is what she told us:

> *"I was sitting in the open-plan co-working space with 20 to 25 colleagues when our manager entered the room. He was showing another man around our office and they were accompanied by one of our senior leaders. I was sitting at my desk, minding my own business, when in front of everyone, he pointed at me and said: 'This is my predecessor's bitch.' They laughed and then moved on."*

This woman was actually the former manager's personal assistant, and although her colleagues were shocked by how she had been spoken to, it was not uncommon. This extremely masculine culture, which we found consistently in the survey results, was why she left.

When we had completed our survey, we could see so many other expressions of that culture in other people's experiences.

Another of the questions we always ask during our inclusion surveys is, "Would you recommend your sister/brother/daughter/son to work at this company?" Probably, the man who was giving the tour in the incident above thought that it was a great place to work, and he most likely recommended working there to everyone in his response to the daughter/son question in the quantitative survey. However, a large majority of the female respondents would recommend their brother or son to work there, but not their daughter or sister. What we found is a perception gap between those with privileges and those without. As in this particular case, if we find a significant difference in how men and women answer this question, we know it is either a very feminine or a very masculine culture.

This episode is an expression of one of the core reasons why diversity has not happened yet. This company, like many other companies, had been

WHY HASN'T THIS HAPPENED ALREADY?

working on creating gender balance and diversity for decades and it had not succeeded because of this toxic culture.

The company in question is a large organisation, with over 20,000 employees. It has ambitions of creating a 50/50 gender balance in the near future, but when we looked at the figures, it was clear that this was unlikely to happen. The numbers revealed that every second woman they hired said she would leave within the first two years of her employment.

When it comes to diversity and inclusion (D&I), we do not recommend having diversity in a company that has no inclusion. It is terrible to be the minority or gender that is not truly accepted. Remember the graphs I shared in the previous chapter? Those demonstrate that having diversity without inclusion is a very bad idea and, as we explored earlier, will actually damage the performance of your business.

The many degrees of inclusion

There was another company that we carried out an inclusion survey for and one of the questions we asked was, "Do all employees, regardless of their background, have the same opportunities for advancing in your company?"

In response, 43% said "No" and 8% said "I don't know". That means over half, 51%, of people working at that company are not convinced that everybody has the same advancement opportunities.

One of the interesting quotes that came out of that survey was from a person who was stuck at a relatively low level within the organisation, despite having been a high performer for many years, because he had an introverted personality and needed time to process his thoughts before sharing them with others. He added that he knew it was not seen as a strength within that company, so it was something he had been trying to work on for years, even though it went against his personal preference.

This is an example of a talented guy trying to change to fit in. He was trying to go from being an introvert to being an extrovert because that was what worked in that company. That person did not feel included and his talent was not recognised, despite the fact that he was a high performer.

This is another issue with having diversity but no inclusivity: you do not see talent if it does not fit into the mould.

45

Diversity is not only about the visible diversity parameters, it is also about diversity of thought. After all, one of the important benefits of diversity is the difference in thoughts, perspectives and opinions it brings. You want people to feel welcome introducing new thoughts and ideas, since this is key to innovation. To do that, you need an inclusive environment for everyone, where it feels safe to share new ideas and question the old. Who is responsible for creating an environment where new ideas are welcomed and innovation flourishes? You can boil it down to one person: the CEO.

In the last chapter, we became familiar with the Nordea/Robert Næss study about the effect of a female CEO, but let me just recap and start with the conclusion: "Companies run by women perform far better than the market."

In 2017 Robert Næss showed us that, after studying 11,000 publicly traded companies, those with a female CEO or a female head of the board of directors had a 25% annualized return (since 2009), more than double the 11% delivered by the MSCI world index. The Nordea team studied companies across industries and geographies in both developed and emerging markets with good liquidity – a trading volume of at least $2 million a day.

Apart from being an amazing eye-opener, this was one of the first studies that really focused on the role of the CEO as an individual power in such a large number of companies.

Now we turn to the important question of why having women at the helm of companies results in higher returns. Næss himself offered a few very plausible reasons. Firstly, considering how difficult it is for a woman to become a CEO or a chairperson, it is most likely that only the very best make it to the top. Another reason might very well be that successful companies are more likely to hire top female executives whereas (as the study states) "struggling companies may go for the 'safe' bet of hiring a man". Thirdly, Næss suggests, women may simply be better managers and more careful, and thus credible, in their projections.

Although I do not doubt any of those explanations, I think it is interesting to take the considerations a few steps further and ask the very interesting question which has everything to do with the subject of this book: what is it that these female top executives can teach their colleagues?

Discussions about the role and importance of the "right" CEO often unfold in connection with salaries and the defense for gilding the best individuals is clear: the importance of the role of the CEO simply cannot be overestimated. I have to say that even if top salaries sometimes seem to be beyond my comprehension, I totally agree. The role of the CEO cannot be overestimated.

All our experience now shows that when female executives, in general, enter a culture and are given space, they are bound to push inclusiveness and diversity, and the more power they possess, the greater the effect. Most women are transformational leaders creating healthy cultures, and by being just that, they add a competitive edge.[1] Therefore, what I am adding to Næss' reasons is that the remarkable results are closely linked to inclusivity, innovation and a welcoming approach to a volatile, uncertain, complex and ambiguous world.

If you ask what colleagues can learn from their female CEOs and chairpersons, I suggest first and foremost this: find the courage to trust that a colourful and more complicated decision landscape is a lot better and more profitable in the long run than putting a lid on creativity and innovation.

By narrowing and silencing the contribution of the business' many talents and points of view, you do not only promote burn-out and exit-urge, which is costly enough on its own, you also simply prevent the culture from doing its best and from achieving outstanding results.

---

[1]McKinsey (2008), "Women Matter – female leadership, a competitive edge for the future".

47

Resistance to being challenged by alternative views and the real multi-layered world, and thus to diversity of thought, can be compared to tunnel vision. A false simplicity is created for which the price is a straitjacket on innovation, constant talent flight and mediocre performance.

Therefore, let me conclude that the significance of the CEO role cannot be overestimated. He or she can and will by his/her behaviour and communication liberate or liquidate the innovative power, the quality of decisions and the sustainability of the culture. D&I-resistant CEOs (or even those who are curious, but still blind to the potential) often want their views to be confirmed, which is why they avoid, freeze out or even fight those who might challenge their worldview by, for instance, asking: what if people find out that we are cheating? The German CEO of Volkswagen might not have been arrested in Miami airport in 2017 for his role in "Emissions-gate" if someone in his team had had the courage to ask that particular question.

D&I-passionate CEOs, on the other hand, appreciate being challenged when confronted with the whole complicated picture, including unanticipated and even provocative views, before they make up their minds.

> *"I realised that men played at home at the top of the business world. The women were welcome to join, but on the men's terms."*
> *– From an interview with Caroline Farberger, CEO at ICA Försäkring AB, after gender reassignment surgery[2]*

---

[2]Mosbech, H. (2020), "'Jeg anede ikke, hvor mange privilegier jeg havde.' Da topchefen skiftede køn og opdagede, at alt, hun troede om ligestilling, var forkert" ("'I had no idea how many privileges I had.' When the CEO changed gender and discovered that everything she thought about equality was wrong"), *Zetland*, 5 September 2020, available at: https://www.zetland.dk/historie/sejvJjNX-moBPQmW4-b2215.

To take this just two steps further: Why are male CEOs in general (and no studies show that this goes only for the elderly guys) less prone to be passionate D&I front runners compared to their female colleagues? I do not know why. However, I do know that once they get it, feel it in their bones and recognise their former blindness and the bottom-line potential of differences, they will want to change things. Then there are those who are waiting for the D&I agenda to go away so that they can get back to business as usual. They do a lot of harm, deliberately standing in the way of the imaginative and multi-talented processes all companies need to embrace future challenges.

One CEO who has unique experience of how male and female CEOs face different challenges is Caroline Farberger, CEO at ICA Försäkring AB, whose quote I shared above. "It felt like a very big experiment", Farberger said, when talking about making the decision to have male to female surgery, and change her first name from Carl to Caroline.[3]

The experiment was this: what would happen when the CEO in a million dollar company one day went home as a man and the next day came to work as a woman in high heels and nail polish?

First of all, Caroline identified a blind spot that Carl had: "I think a lot of men are not aware of the effect of their behaviour. They think they are working for equality, but subconsciously pull their behaviour in the opposite direction. You think you have equality because there are three women and three men in management, but you do not have that if you only look at the men when you ask for views – if you really only listen to the men."

---

[3]Mosbech, H. (2020), "'Jeg anede ikke, hvor mange privilegier jeg havde.' Da topchefen skiftede køn og opdagede, at alt, hun troede om ligestilling, var forkert" ("'I had no idea how many privileges I had.' When the CEO changed gender and discovered that everything she thought about equality was wrong"), *Zetland*, 5 September 2020, available at: https://www.zetland.dk/historie/sejvJjNX-moBPQmW4-b2215.

"When I was a man it was my perception that we had an even playing field. I thought everyone played on their home ground. That we had gender equality," she says today. "I didn't see there was a problem."

She is convinced that the companies that actually are capable of including *all* kinds of people have a head start and a competitive advantage over their competitors. ICA Forsäkring has for years been the fastest growing insurance company in Sweden. "Inclusion in business is a launch pad to success," Caroline Farberger says.

> *"There are no creative people where I'm working... but there could be, and we could improve and do better with a more innovative way of thinking."*
>
> *– Male respondent to an inclusion survey*

Organisational inclusivity is a fundamental factor

Both of these stories highlight the need for organisational inclusivity. This is a fundamental factor in the retention of diverse talent at a business. As Verna Myers, VP, Inclusion Strategy at Netflix, said: "Diversity is being asked to the party, inclusion is being asked to dance."[4]

It is terrible to be invited to a party where no one wants to dance with you, and that analogy is the essence of diversity without inclusion. Both the companies whose stories I have shared so far in this chapter had invited people to the party but they were not asked to dance. Both companies made the classic mistake of focusing on diversity instead of inclusion.

---

[4]Myers, V. (2017), "Diversity Doesn't Stick Without Inclusion", *Vernamyers.com*, 4 February 2017, available at: https://www.vernamyers.com/2017/02/04/diversity-doesnt-stick-without-inclusion/.

That meant they had implemented recruitment processes to improve gender balance and increase the number of people from minority groups who were hired, but this did not last and those people left. Look back at that first example: at entry level, they were achieving gender balance but, as our inclusion survey showed, every second woman who was employed would leave within two years.

Focus on the human

Another unintended factor of focusing too much on diversity parameters when hiring is that you put people in a box when you hire them because of their gender, age, skin colour, nationality, sexual orientation, disability and so on. No one is only the colour of their skin, or their gender, or their nationality; there is so much more to being human.

To focus on just those diversity parameters ignores the complexity of what it is to be human. It can also give the person who is hired the impression that they only got the job because they fitted into one of those boxes that their employer needed to tick. This is not conducive to creating a feeling of belonging.

Hiring someone because they are part of a particular minority group is called tokenism.[5]

One of the things we always find through our inclusion surveys is that those who contribute to tokenism are blissfully unaware of it. This is an observation, I am not apportioning blame. It is simply the nature of privilege; it makes you blind.

---

[5]See Bohnet, I. (2016), *What Works: Gender Equality by Design*, Harvard University Press.

This is also part of being human. We still have our "Stone Age" brains, where we think that if we are okay and our tribe is okay then everything is fine. We have this built-in "them-and-us" mechanism, which means that everything different from us is a threat and that inviting *the other* in is courageous.

It is only when we become really conscious of these matters that we can sense the pain this causes others and become more aware of it.

The challenge is that we, as human beings, only really understand things by experiencing what they feel like. Because this is how we learn, at the Living Institute we make sure our workshops are very experiential. In these workshops, we give people the experience of what it means to lose privileges and power and how it feels to be *the other*. This experience often makes people misty eyed, because then they finally understand what it means to be different and to not have that difference accepted. Sometimes we facilitate these experiential Power Dynamics workshops for participants belonging to what could be considered the most privileged group of people on Earth: global executives on MBA programmes. The goal of this experiential workshop is to create behavioural change in their leadership style.

James Baldwin, writing passionately about racial discrimination, puts it this way: "I can't believe what you say, because I see what you do."[6]

Diversity vs inclusion

Understanding the difference between diversity and inclusion is essential, as you can see from these examples. None of the companies I have given as examples here had inclusive cultures where everybody felt they belonged and were included and felt psychologically safe.

---

[6]Baldwin, J. (1966), "A Report from Occupied Territory", *The Nation*, 11 July 1966, available at: https://www.thenation.com/article/archive/report-occupied-territory/.

At the company from the first example I shared, the women who worked there were exhausted by the toxic episodes like the one I described. The culture was extremely competitive. Long hours were a source of pride. Career paths were unclear. Promotions were often decided in closed "boys' networks". Innovation, diversity of thought and new ideas were not welcomed. There are still no women on their executive committee although HR had, for decades, introduced countless D&I initiatives, with no effect.

Striving for diversity but failing to consider inclusion is one of the main reasons why we have not seen greater progress in this area among businesses. This creates fatigue.

Companies are trying, but…

Many companies started the journey towards a perfect gender balance and full inclusion of all minorities decades ago, and most of them have failed.

Despite introducing a series of D&I initiatives over the course of decades, women and minorities are still minorities in practically all Fortune 500 companies. We are still looking for a "superhero" company that has achieved it, even though there are some, like IKEA, that are close.

> *"The debate we have had on gender equality for many years has been wrong. It has become a statistics game. What percentage of top executives are women? But we do not get to change anything until we really talk about inclusion."*
> *— From an interview with Caroline Farberger, CEO at ICA Försäkring AB, after gender reassignment surgery[7]*

---

[7]Mosbech, H. (2020), "'Jeg anede ikke, hvor mange privilegier jeg havde.' Da topchefen skiftede køn og opdagede, at alt, hun troede om ligestilling, var forkert" ("'I had no idea how many privileges I had.' When the CEO changed gender and discovered that everything she thought about equality was wrong"), *Zetland*, 5 September 2020, available at: https://www.zetland.dk/historie/sejvJjNX-moBPQmW4-b2215.

The difficulty is that most of the initiatives that have been implemented have had no, or very little, provable effects in that period. As a result, when the HR team is ready with a new series of initiatives, these are often met with fatigue and resistance within the organisation.

This is not only because people have had enough of initiatives and solutions that have no effect, but also because the solutions being presented are not perceived to be relevant to the individual employee or manager. This is typically true for both the privileged and not so privileged within the organisation.

Let us look at the company from that first example again, which might decide that it is going to create a female network. However, the women joining the female network are shocked to hear that they are not the only ones experiencing such unacceptable incidents – in fact, every woman in the room has had similar experiences, or has witnessed them, so more women decide to leave the company. In this instance, introducing female networks does the opposite of solving the gender equation.

Similarly, the behaviour of the male manager who was giving the office tour will not change because his female colleagues are invited to female-only events after hours. He is not part of the equation.

Rather than creating a female network, it would make much more sense to mobilise the manager and his male colleagues, thereby changing the paradigms for acceptable behaviours and ensuring the culture is conducive to retaining their female colleagues. Later in the book, we will take a deeper look at how you can mobilise men at your organisation and why this is fundamental to the success of D&I initiatives.

Why do HR teams and others within organisations continue to introduce initiatives that everyone in an organisation views as irrelevant? Because these initiatives to create gender balance and inclusion are not based on data, they are based on guesswork – and this is another reason why so many of these initiatives fail.

As I touched upon in Chapter 2, this issue is always classed as business critical by top management. If an issue is characterised as such, it follows that a strategy has to be put in place to solve the problem and challenges. Think for a moment about other business-critical issues and the strategies organisations put in place to tackle them: how many of those strategies are based on guessing? The answer is not many, because that is not normally how you form a strategy to tackle a business-critical challenge.

Businesses need to understand that having this deliberate roadmap of steps is essential to ensure the survival of the company in the long run. They cannot do this without collecting relevant data and creating a baseline analysis of the current level of inclusion and diversity. When you have this data, you can identify focal areas and build a roadmap to implement the most impactful initiatives.

All of this is based on the results from the analysis of the data from the inclusion survey. Monitoring the outcomes and results of the initiatives is equally important and ideally will be carried out annually. This allows a business to set new goals and adjust its initiatives so that they have the highest impact and evolve as the company develops. Taking these steps, and getting it right this time, makes a huge difference to a company's approach and the buy-in to D&I initiatives.

Are you asking the right questions?

At the Living Institute, I cannot think of any company we have worked with that has had this baseline inclusion data when we first met them. None of them had conducted in-depth inclusion surveys like the ones we carry out.

In many cases, these companies do run workplace wellbeing and engagement surveys every year, but these do not measure the level of belonging, inclusion and psychological safety among their employees and, therefore, they do not uncover these discrepancies between the level of inclusion and the initiatives they are already implementing.

In fact, when we carry out our inclusion survey, we often find that the initiatives that businesses have already implemented have made things worse, and the ones that would have made the difference were not even considered. This is the result of basing decisions on guesswork rather than data.

Are you running a marathon or starting a sprint?

Before we start working with any business, we always ask HR whether they have just embarked on this journey towards diversity and inclusion, or if they have made earlier attempts. Nine times out of 10 we are told this is the third, fourth or even fifth time that they have launched a new D&I programme. Some of our clients have been trying to create better diversity and inclusion for 20+ years. We even had one client recently who told us they had been trying to create gender balance for 50 years.

Next we ask, "Would you characterise your efforts as a marathon, where you haven't reached the finishing line yet? If you've been running a marathon for 50 years, you may have run backwards a couple of times. You've probably been lost along the way and taken a few wrong turns too. If you've been running for all of this time and you still can't see the finish line, would you rather make it into a sprint. Going fast from A to Z by getting every step right?"

Most of the people we speak to are keen to turn this marathon into a sprint, because now the ground is burning beneath their feet. As we have seen, those in top management know this is business critical, so taking action is important.

What is important to understand is that if you want to turn this into a sprint, you have to do everything differently to the way you are doing it right now.

This means clearly defining roles and who is responsible for the whole project. It means understanding what resources are required, as well as building a strategy to make a change and turn that long, meandering marathon into a straight sprint. It means understanding that every step counts.

Top management has to walk the talk

Another reason why D&I initiatives have been unsuccessful in the past is that, for them to work, there needs to be synchronisation within those in top management.

Often we find that two out of five executives, for example, have seen the light and truly believe in the power of inclusion and belonging. They know that inclusion and diversity is critical to the company's survival in a VUCA (volatile, uncertain, complex and ambiguous) world and the Fourth Industrial Revolution. Businesses were already operating in a world of uncertainty where everything was extremely complex, and then Covid-19 came along.

Nobody knows what will come along next to derail your company or your strategy completely. All we do know is that everything will change. This is the world you have to navigate as an executive. The future belongs to those who manage to do so.

Now, for two of our five executives, the primary reason to have diversity of thought within their organisation is to survive in this VUCA world. They are the ones who say that diversity and inclusion is a business-critical issue. However, the other three do not entirely buy into this vision. It might be nice to have but, in their opinion, it is not business critical.

Like ostriches, they hide their heads in the sand hoping that they can reproduce the past and keep on using the tools they already know. These three executives may support window-dressing initiatives, but they are very much ticking the box. This is not enough to create a cultural revolution. A cultural revolution requires a break with old habits and sameness-thinking.

There are many symptoms of this lack of acceptance of the need for wholesale change, such as those in top management appointing people who look exactly like them as the next in line. This is very demoralising and results in other people who do not conform to that "image" leaving the business and joining companies with a compelling D&I vision. Who are they, the ones leaving to work for a more attractive company? They are the young, talented individuals and the ambitious women that any employer would dream of having on their team. If that is not harmful enough, it might be one of your competitors that lures them away.

This means that you are left with the people who are thriving in this work environment and who do not have a problem fitting in or finding role models in the existing management team. Or even worse, they are ones who are stuck because they cannot get a job in other companies.

It is, essentially, a "mini-me" syndrome, where some executives tell themselves, "This guy is so intelligent, right for the job and competent..." and what they often do not recognise, or say, is, "...and he looks exactly like me".

A couple of years ago we carried out an inclusion survey at a company in the tanker industry. Before the survey, we were told that there was no need for any D&I initiatives and that they had it covered. When the results of the online survey ticked in, 92% of the respondents said that the executive committee was not doing enough to act on diversity and inclusion. You can window dress and communicate that it is very important all you want, but people can sense when you are not walking the talk.

A synchronised executive committee is 100% committed and aligned on the potential of diversity and inclusion, and they walk the talk until it is done.

> *"This is a very masculine company run by white male engineers in their fifties. I am surrounded by brilliant, ambitious women but they are completely invisible to management. Therefore I am happy that they have finally asked us how we perceive the level of D&I – it's long overdue. However, if this is not backed up by ground-breaking changes, I'll leave in eight months and become a stay-at-home dad, letting my wife have her dream career. I really need to see our CEO get up there and talk passionately about these matters – or I am out of here."*
>
> *– Male leader of leaders in an inclusion survey in 2020*

Something doesn't add up

The next reason why things have not already changed is that most CFOs have not done the math. I outlined the business case in the last chapter, but take the time to do the math and create a comprehensive business case for your organisation.

For example, what exactly is it going to cost you when every second talented team member walks out of your organisation within two years of being employed? Let us say you have 200 young, talented individuals in your high potential programme and you now know that 50% will leave you within the next couple of years.

It is going to cost you at least twice their annual salary to find a replacement and get them up to speed, and that is a low estimate. In many cases it would be fair to say it will cost you five times their annual salary to do this.

The next question you have to ask is, "What price are we going to pay when our competitors outperform us by having cracked the code to mirror the market because they have no problem hiring and retaining talent?"

Your competitors could be stealing your customers or even stealing your talent, all simply because they are more innovative, inclusive and fun to work for than you.

When you are doing the math, you also have to allocate a budget to improving diversity and inclusion. We are often approached by heads of diversity and inclusion, members of diversity councils and HR professionals who want to know the price of a half-day training session in unconscious bias. Once we have agreed on a price, they tell us they will have to get back to us once they, hopefully, are granted the money from someone above.

When we ask them why they want to offer unconscious bias training and whether it is part of a series of initiatives, all too often the answer is, "Top management has decided we should have gender balance at all levels by 2025 and we have been tasked with making that happen. We do not actually have a budget, but we might get some budget for half a day of unconscious bias training."

Half a day of training will not be enough to create the cultural revolution that is required to meet such an ambitious goal. These companies will not succeed if they do not base their initiatives on a strategy, a roadmap and a budget reflecting what it takes to make a cultural transformation.

They skipped three very important steps and went directly to step four by reaching out for an initiative to randomly implement. I will explain all four of these steps in the next chapter.

How to start your cultural revolution

Once your executive committee is synchronised and has uncovered what elements in the culture created the problem in the first place, you have to be very clear about the consequences of *not* making changes to make your organisation more diverse and inclusive. The executive committee must, in unison, establish *why* this is business critical. It could be a statement along the lines of: "We will be out of business in five years if we don't make radical changes, because this is how much money we are losing every month, every year, due to the fact that we haven't cracked the code yet. At the same time, our competitors have!"

Do the math: count by count, dollar by dollar, yen by yen. You will see the figures stacking up in favour of greater diversity and inclusivity. Allocate a suitable budget that will finance any necessary initiatives and enable you to create a true cultural transformation, based, of course, on data pointing you in the right direction, rather than on guesswork.

Focus on inclusion rather than diversity.

Ten reasons why this hasn't happened already

I have outlined the main reasons why so many organisations are still struggling with diversity and inclusion. To clearly demonstrate why this has not happened already, below is a list of 10 things that are happening in many organisations around the world, all of which prevent the kind of cultural revolution we have been talking about and that is essential for a company's survival:

1. Failing to anchor responsibility at the top.
2. Focusing on diversity instead of inclusion.
3. Underestimating what it takes to achieve a cultural transformation by eliminating the barriers in the existing culture that prevented you from achieving your goals earlier.
4. Appointing task forces and support groups that are not educated in the fundamentals of how to create a culture of inclusion.
5. Basing inclusion and diversity initiatives on guesses and hunches and what other companies do rather than data from your own organisation.
6. Underestimating the budget required for a deep cultural transformation or, even worse, allocating no budget at all.
7. Failing to monitor the development and results of the recommended initiatives systematically every year.
8. Reproducing worst practices believing they are best practices.
9. Increasing existing fatigue by introducing yet another series of initiatives with no measurable impact.
10. Failing to mobilise and educate everyone, especially leaders at all levels, to reach these goals.

Remembering diversity is different to equality

Equality is an important concept to embrace when working to create a more diverse and inclusive environment, but we also need to be aware of the distinctions between diversity, inclusivity and equality.

What characterises a company that is truly diverse and highly inclusive is that everyone is valued, respected and heard. Everybody feels like they belong, they can speak their minds and contribute freely with their ideas. This only happens when each individual feels they can authentically be themselves.

If we are all equal, that means we are all allowed to touch the ball when we are playing a game, for instance. If you look at homogenous countries like Denmark, you could say that we have had equality for the last 100 years, with women being allowed to vote and work and so on. However, the problem with equality is that it is sometimes mistaken for sameness.

It comes down to the idea that you have to be the same as me and that makes us equal. However, at the heart of diversity is the concept of not being the same. Diversity is about feeling comfortable being as different as we are as human beings. It is equality without sameness.

Looking for sameness and mistaking it for equality is another of the barriers we face in improving diversity as well. Basically, we need to celebrate our differences – the more the merrier.

Summary

We have looked at the many reasons why there has not been a greater shift towards diversity and inclusion within many organisations and I outlined 10 things that I highly recommend you avoid. Now that you have seen the business case and understand why you may have struggled with D&I initiatives in your business in the past, let us move on to what you *can* and *should* do.

In the rest of this book, we are going to dig deeper into each of the areas discussed in this chapter to help you find a blueprint for starting your own cultural transformation and creating a diverse and inclusive environment.

Part 2

How to Reach Diversity Intelligence

In Chapter 3, I shared a number of reasons why there is not greater diversity and inclusivity within many of the world's businesses. Although there are many reasons why this has not happened yet, one of the most common issues we encounter is that businesses start their efforts in the wrong place.

We have identified four steps that companies need to take in order to create a diverse and inclusive environment, which are shown in the Figure 12.1.

"Give us a half-day unconscious bias workshop!"

In our experience, too many companies start at Step 4: Action, but in bypassing the first three steps of the process, any training or other initiatives they introduce generally will not have a lasting impact. Once you get back to your desk after the training, all the cultural barriers are still in place, ready to kill your enthusiasm for making the necessary changes.

Let us break down those four steps and explore why each is important and why it is vital to tackle them in the right order.

Step 1: Drive

As already mentioned, when we ask those in top management why they want to embark on this journey, one or two say that it is business critical to improve diversity and inclusivity at their organisation. Saying that it is a business-critical issue is not enough, though. In the C-suite they need to find out *why* D&I is business critical and what is driving their belief that it is business critical.

Each organisation also needs to uncover to whom it is important and why. Is it important to your clients and customers? Is it important to your employees who will leave the company if they do not see a change? Is it important to the bottom line? Do those in management want to see the financial upsides of improved D&I?

When we encourage the C-suite to clarify where this drive for better diversity and inclusivity comes from, we typically find that it matters in all aspects of the company. This is also an opportunity to identify any areas of resistance, or potential board members who do not understand just how business critical a lack of diversity and inclusivity really is.

When we finish this exercise, we see a shift in perspective from those in top management positions. Not only is diversity and inclusivity a business-critical issue, but it is *business critical* in that it is a matter of survival.

With that realisation comes a temptation to throw initiatives at the issue. There may even be a tendency to panic at this stage, but it is important not to rush ahead. You have to move calmly on to Step 2.

Step 2: Knowledge

Whatever action you take at your organisation to improve diversity and inclusivity needs to be based on data from the organisation itself. It is important to know what exactly is going on and who in your business feels included and who does not. What characterises those who do not feel included? Is it their skin colour, age, gender, educational background, faith, sexual orientation or something else? How big is the pocket of resistance within the wider organisation? Who will leave the business if you do not change?

Instead of trying to fix everything, gathering this data allows you to understand what it is that actually needs to be fixed and what initiatives need to be put in place. You have to learn what people are saying about diversity and inclusivity at your organisation. Finding the painful stories is just as important as collecting the numbers, because these also give you a clear picture of where to start. These stories give you an understanding of what it is like to be in someone else's shoes.

When you have this data, you can use it to back up your strategy when you are confronted with resistance from pockets in your organisation. The fundamental argument may be that improving D&I is a good thing to do, but if you can meet resistance with arguments such as, "Our competitors have innovated more than we have" or "We are losing talent crucial to the running of the business", and support those arguments with data, you will see that resistance decreases.

Carrying out a baseline inclusion survey across your organisation is not only important to mobilising everyone and building your strategy, but also for monitoring progress as you move forward.

You also need to find out how quickly you need to move forward. Ask where your organisation wants to be two, five and 10 years from now. Once you know where the problems lie and how quickly you need to deal with them, you can move on to Step 3.

Step 3: Strategy

This step involves exploring how to change the culture that created the problem in the first place. It involves deciding how the different levels of the organisation will be involved in this journey, which I will discuss in greater detail in Chapter 4 when I talk about roles and responsibilities.

After completing Steps 1 and 2, you will have the goals that you are striving to achieve and you will have a timeframe for achieving them. Step 3 is where you figure out the how: what initiatives do you need to implement for each of those goals and who will be involved and when will the initiatives happen?

For instance, if managers are not provided with new tools for their toolbox, then they will keep leading the way they always have. Everyone has to be equipped with the tools and knowledge they need in order to make that cultural transformation.

Our data may show that women are more ambitious than men. Why do we then spend time and money on female-only leadership programmes instead of simply promoting the ambitious women we already have?

Our data may show that 60% of the female leaders say there is enough female talent inside the organisation, but only 20% of the male leaders can see them. In this case, let us focus on mobilising men until 60% of the male leaders also see the female talent that is already there.

Creating this strategy is essential to ensure that you are focusing your efforts in the right places, with the right people, at the right time and providing the appropriate resources to bring about meaningful and sustainable cultural change. Only once you have this strategy in place do you move to Step 4.

Step 4: Action

This is when you act on what you now know. Having this drive, knowledge and strategy in place means you know exactly who needs to do what, as well as what training and initiatives are required at what levels, to synchronise the whole organisation around this drive for change.

At the heart of the action is the understanding that your business may not exist five years from now if this does not happen. This is where you mobilise everyone, at every level, to bring about the necessary cultural change to improve diversity and inclusivity.

It is essential to measure and monitor the changes that occur as you, step by step, introduce your initiatives and training. You will notice that the diagram I shared at the start of this part of the book is circular, which is deliberate because you do not complete Steps 1 to 4 and then stop. You monitor, adjust and check again, and you keep going around this wheel to keep the agenda alive until your data shows that everything is fixed.

Putting the wheel into practice

In this part of the book, I will share practical advice for implementing the wheel at your organisation. We will start by looking at roles and responsibilities in Chapter 4, before going into detail about how to achieve synchronisation across the executive team.

From there, in Chapter 6, we will explore in more detail how to back up your D&I strategies with data, and then look at the many practical ways that you can roll out a D&I strategy within your organisation. This includes running inclusive leadership training, the need to train D&I Champions, and when and how to introduce unconscious bias training at your organisation.

I will also explore cultural intelligence and show you how you can develop this essential skill and will finish Part 2 by examining how to create gender balance within organisations, explaining the importance of mobilising men in particular.

Slowly but surely we are applying diversity intelligence and putting your company on the right track towards a brighter future.

Chapter 4

Roles and Responsibilities

Where to start

The role of HR within a cultural transformation is incredibly important. These are the people you will want to support and push forward this agenda, but they need to stand on a different platform. Instead of starting in HR, we have to start where it all begins and that is in top management.

What are your company's core values?

In the 1990s, most organisations defined their core values. These are the core pillars of an organisation's identity and they are rooted within that company's DNA. Everyone in that business had to pledge allegiance to the values and live by them; if you did not, then you did not work at that company.

The majority of companies introduced value-based leadership in this period and therefore leaders know how to understand the value proposition and how to filter it down through the organisation. Inclusion and diversity

Clearing the hallways

This is a story about a woman who was appointed to create gender balance across all levels of a large financial institution, from the C-suite down. There are 30,000 employees at this bank and it is certainly what you could describe as a Sisyphean task. There was no way she would succeed. Like the Greek myth, she was pushing that stone up the mountain, only to see it roll back down time and time again. In short, she was set up to fail.

Yet her job was to create gender balance within the organisation. It is what her KPIs were based on, but she was not given any power to change things and she had no budget. After 13 years she was allowed to go and of course the company hired someone to replace her but without making any material changes to their approach.

The reason I called this story *Clearing the hallways* is that after about 10 years in this job, the woman noticed that everybody would try to avoid meeting her in the hallways because she was always thought of as bad news. She would ask managers how things were progressing in their departments and offer to run workshops and so on, but no one wanted to listen.

She said that people would seem to jump into the closest office just to avoid meeting her, because they simply did not want to hear more about diversity and inclusion.

Research has even shown that women and members of minority groups who engage in diversity-valuing behaviour are frequently penalised for it.[1]

What this story tells us is that there is a tendency to appoint people who do not have the knowledge and resources to create the necessary cultural transformation. I trained the woman in this story, so I know she was not an expert in this field when she was appointed to the job. She was also very young and put in a position without power and real influence. Ironically, this young, inexperienced woman was supposed, on her own, to create gender balance at all levels within the organisation, including the all-male executive

---

[1]Johnson, S.K., and Hekman, D. (2016), "Women and Minorities Are Penalized for Promoting Diversity", *Harvard Business Review*, 23 March 2016, available at: https://hbr.org/2016/03/women-and-minorities-are-penalized-for-promoting-diversity.

team. This is how this particular organisation chose to approach the issue and bring about a cultural transformation.

Sadly, it is a story we encounter all too often in our work at the Living Institute. It is the wrong approach in every way: it is bad for her, it is bad for the company, it is bad for the agenda and you achieve absolutely nothing by doing this.

need to be encompassed in these core values and the guidelines and principles that organisations use to define how they conduct their business. In doing so, this message can trickle down and influence all the decision-making processes within an organisation.

Making a cultural transformation towards inclusivity requires a very similar approach.

Why you have to walk the talk

Moving towards improved diversity and inclusivity backfires when companies simply window dress, when those in the top management positions fail to walk the talk.

At the end of 2020 there was a very high-profile example of what happens when diversity and inclusivity are not deeply rooted in the values but are rather just a matter of ticking the box. Dr Timnit Gebru, who was the technical co-lead for Google's Ethical Artificial Intelligence team, was forced out of the company. In an email[2] she wrote to colleagues at the company before being fired, she said, "Your life gets worse when you start advocating for underrepresented people, you start making the other leaders upset."

[2]Newton, C. (2020), "The withering email that got an ethical AI researcher fired at Google", *Platformer*, 3 December 2020, available at: https://www.platformer. news/p/the-withering-email-that-got-an-ethical.

Dr Gebru also stated that there is "zero accountability" and said, "There is no way more documents or more conversations will achieve anything." She finished her email by stressing the importance of making changes in leadership to make changes to the culture.

Her email speaks of the lack of accountability and incentives in relation to D&I initiatives, but also the fatigue that many who are fighting for better inclusivity and diversity experience when they are faced with a lack of willingness to change and a lack of true accountability from the top.

What makes this story more shocking is the reason she lost her job. Dr Gebru was working on research, along with a number of colleagues at Google and other academic experts, into facial recognition AI and the biases this technology has against black people. What led to her losing her job was a dispute with Google's management over this research.

Instead of acting on what Dr Gebru and other researchers found, which is an issue that is incredibly important to correct, Google fired her; the person who brought the message that something needed to change. At the same time, those in top management at Google are still saying that they are supporting diversity and inclusivity. When stories like this emerge though, the organisation loses all credibility both internally and externally.

The only right way for the top management team at Google, or any other organisation, to act is to always support the agenda and back up the whistleblowers fighting to improve things. If management does not do this, nobody will believe them when they say they want to see greater diversity and inclusion in their organisation and that it has high priority. As you can see from this example at Google, you can lose everything when top management is not synchronised on the issue.

The role of the CEO in D&I initiatives

The CEO plays a crucial role in embedding D&I at the heart of an organisation. The CEO's role is to synchronise his or her management team, as well as to build a strong, ambitious and radical inclusion of diversity strategy, with clear goals and fixed timeframes that are based on data from their organisation.

It is also important for the CEO to anchor the agenda in the C-suite, either by taking full responsibility or by making one of the CXOs responsible for driving the agenda forward. They also have to appoint a powerful task force of experts, who will implement the strategy step by step, as well as measure and monitor progress and adjust focal areas moving forward.

We recommend monitoring developments and hosting weekly follow-up meetings between the task force and the CXO who is responsible for implementing the D&I strategy.

Dr Gebru used the phrase "zero accountability" in relation to how D&I is handled by top management at Google. That is a place where you do not want your company to be.

The role of the board

Along with the CEO, the board also plays an important role in embedding D&I initiatives into an organisation. As we discovered in the first part of the book, the urgency to improve diversity and inclusivity often comes from the board, rather than the CEO, since the board members' primary role is to make the shareholders happy by safeguarding the maximum return of their shares.

"We need a sprint, not a marathon"

This story is about the new head of D&I at a multi-national telecommunications company, who was asked to design a D&I strategy and present it to the board of directors. In this organisation, D&I was at an embryonic stage and there was a widespread indifference towards it, as well as some resistance.

This new head of D&I took a rather conciliatory approach and was attempting not to offend or put pressure on anyone. At this time, women and minority groups had occasionally expressed that they were painfully aware that there was an exclusionary culture, as well as a "them-and-us" tendency within the company. Many of these people covered important sides of themselves at work to fit in.

However, the new head of D&I was also new to the topic, coming from a traditional HR background. It was a steep learning curve for him and he reached out in his HR networks to ask what initiatives others had introduced. He blindly groped towards which initiatives to recommend, and then developed the D&I programme based on what he discovered from his enquiries with his HR networks. He presented this strategy to the board, envisioning that it would do the job.

The board at this company was rather international. There were a couple of female board members, as well as a male board member, who had deep knowledge about how to enhance inclusivity and diversity. They were also aware of the commercial imperative.

When the rather nervous head of D&I finished presenting his strategy to the board, he was met with silence. You could have heard a pin drop in the room. At last, one of the board members said, "You need to go back and start all over again. What we need is not a D&I marathon that gets us nowhere, but a sprint to reach ambitious goals in no time."

The board recognised that the programme they had been presented with would not only achieve nothing, but would also lead to the business suffering for many years to come.

Time has run out

This story highlights the common problem that often the people who are tasked with taking the lead on diversity and inclusion do not have the skills or competencies required to make the necessary changes to an organisation. This is why we recommend having D&I Champions who know what they are doing and therefore can make things happen fast.

It is not a secret to anyone that many companies are struggling to reach their goals, while women and minorities are leaving them in high numbers. It is also not a secret that, for decades, most of these companies have introduced half-hearted programmes and action plans containing initiatives that had little or no effect on improving inclusion. The organisation is exhausted and not happy to be faced with yet another attempt.

There is no time for this any more. Following #MeToo and Black Lives Matter, it is clear that younger generations have lost patience with these companies, much like Dr Timnit Gebru at Google.

At the Living Institute, more and more of our clients are telling us that they used to be the most attractive workplace for young talent and the top students leaving university, but now those people do not even want to talk to them, let alone apply for jobs with them.

In this day and age, you have one shot to get this right and practically no time when it comes to hitting the bull's eye. Therefore, anchoring the business-critical D&I agenda in HR is misplaced. It has to be anchored in the C-suite and *supported* by HR champions who have an educational and professional background in D&I. These are what we call D&I Champions and they support all the functions of the organisation in reaching the inclusion goals set out by the C-suite and the board.

The role of D&I Champions

One of the most imperative tasks for D&I Champions is optimising the recruitment process to promote diversity and gender balance and to minimise the structural barriers and biases throughout the organisation.

How can D&I Champions approach this?

In collaboration with key people from HR, the D&I Champions can review critical processes influencing gender balance and diversity in management, such as:

- Creating transparency in the occupation of positions and career development by busting bias and excluding unintentional, counterproductive cultural traits in recruitment, retention, career planning, performance reviews, talent and high potential programmes, mentoring, exit and post-exit interviews.
- Offering managers access to inclusive leadership programmes, enabling leaders and managers to avoid the old discrimination pitfalls through bias-free, one-to-one employer/manager meetings.
- Informing external recruitment agencies about the business-critical gender balance goals and requiring them to present qualified male and female candidates for all vacant positions.

How to choose a D&I Champion

Most D&I Champions are female, and in fact many are women of colour. However, research shows they are often penalised for being in this role and they face a tough job if they are not given the support and power to make changes.[3]

---

[3]Johnson, S.K., and Hekman, D. (2016), "Women and Minorities Are Penalized for Promoting Diversity", *Harvard Business Review*, 23 March 2016, available at: https://hbr.org/2016/03/women-and-minorities-are-penalized-for-promoting-diversity.

However, in my experience, the best D&I Champions I have ever worked with are those white males who have seen the light and have been on the other side. It might be because they have daughters, a different sexual orientation or have had an experience that has shown them why millennials are staying away from companies without diversity and inclusion.

Often they are extremely passionate but, unlike their female and minority counterparts, it is usually easier for them to get the budget and support they need. Crucially, they are also generally not penalised for working in this role in the same way that women or people of colour are, as the study shows us.

As you heard in the first story I shared in this chapter, women and minorities working in these roles can sometimes lose their jobs for having been unable to create results, usually through no fault of their own, or will most likely be stigmatised and see colleagues avoid meeting them in the hallways.

This simply highlights the importance of empowering your D&I Champions, whoever they are. Ideally, you want them to sit in the diversity intelligence task force owned by the CEO or another C-suite member and be given the power they need in order to succeed. I will talk about D&I Champions in much greater detail in Chapter 8.

The importance of developing inclusive leadership

All leaders must attend mandatory leadership programmes where they develop the tools and skills to execute inclusive leadership.

Think back to the wheel diagram with the four steps that I shared at the beginning of this part of the book. Imagine that your organisation skips Steps 1 to 3 and goes straight to Step 4 by providing anyone who is interested with unconscious bias training. This training allows a large portion of the employees at your organisation to understand the mechanisms of power, how we all have preferences and biases and how we often subconsciously discriminate against others.

Everyone who has attended that training suddenly sees it all the time, because once you begin to understand how these mechanisms work, you see them everywhere. It is incredibly frustrating when this is not followed up with action from everyone at the organisation. It is terrible to have that knowledge and then see everything just continue as it always has; it is like watching the movie *Groundhog Day* on repeat.

Imagine now that you have a department of 50 people who have all had unconscious bias training, but the team leader did not attend the training and does not have inclusion skills. As a result, he or she keeps the old culture alive by leading the way they have always done and thus repeating the past. In a team with that dynamic, you would very likely see more people leaving the company because there is a lack of change.

As you can see, having any D&I agenda without including leadership is damaging. In order to act and lead inclusively, upper and middle management personnel must be trained, otherwise the cocooning tendency of power[4] will simply prevail.

The cocooning tendency of power refers to how leaders include and exclude certain people in the team. Due to time pressures, leaders form

---

[4]Bear Graen, G., and Uhl-Bien, M. (1995), "Relationship-Based Approach to Leadership", *The Leadership Quarterly*, 6(2):219–247, doi: 10.1016/1048-9843(95)90036-5, available at: https://www.researchgate.net/publication/222734345_Relationship-Based_Approach_to_Leadership_Development_of_Leader-Member_Exchange_LMX_Theory_of_Leadership_over_25_Years_Applying_a_Multi-Level_Multi-Domain_Perspective.

a special relationship with a small group of followers – the so-called "in group". This "in group" is trusted and gets more time and attention from the leaders, getting the interesting assignments while having more time and exchanges with them.

Everyone else falls into the "out group", which gets less of the leaders' attention, tends to have a more formal relationship with them, and is involved in fewer exchanges with them. Leaders pick "in group" members relatively early on in the relationship and this group remains relatively stable over time.

This means that new leadership behaviour is a required condition for change. Introducing inclusive leadership programmes will result in a focus on promoting the talent and high potential already present within an organisation, and thereby avoid reverse quotas and unconsciously preferring traditional male behaviour. Through this training, managers are turned into role models and front runners for an inclusive corporate culture. I will explore inclusive leadership training in greater detail in Chapter 7.

How you can develop inclusive leadership

- Include mandatory inclusion modules and training to strengthen diversity and equality cognition and competencies into existing leadership programmes. For any managers who have already participated in these programmes without the diversity dimensions, provide these elements as an add-on.
- Learning to systematically address unconscious bias in decision-making needs to be a fundamental part of any inclusion modules.
- Other mandatory and connected subjects that it is important to cover include age, cultural background, ethnicity, sexual orientation, religion and cultural intelligence, especially for organisations that operate internationally.

The role of communication

When I talk about roles in moving the D&I agenda forward, it is not only roles in terms of jobs, but also the importance of other factors. Communication is particularly vital, and as we saw from the Google example, not only in terms of communicating within your organisation but also in terms of the brand and image of the company.

Too many top managers only pay lip service to diversity and inclusion. Many say that they really want to make changes but then nothing happens, you do not see any action from them and they fail to support people when there are issues.

Clear communication in terms of D&I is twofold. Firstly, it is essential that you tell the good stories and show where you are making progress. Secondly, you have to avoid the "shit storms" that paint the company in a bad light and make people lose faith in your D&I initiatives.

The reason good stories are essential when you are working towards diversity is that hearing before-and-after stories can keep you going. They can show you that there is light at the end of the tunnel. Communicating internally and externally about the effects of your culture change efforts can boost morale, maintain commitment and create a healthier environment overall.

How to use communications to drive your D&I agenda

Effective communication is known to negate myths and bust stereotypes. The following are the kinds of stories you can share to help with this:

- Stories about role models, men and women.
- Stories about women making it.
- Stories about the new bias-free recruitment and promotion practices.

- Stories about men and women working their way across organisational silos.
- Messages from those in top management committing to gender balance and better representation of minorities at all levels.
- Anti-stereotypes that picture a diverse talent pool of different ages, genders, ethnicities and life phases – the obvious example being a man taking care of his kids.

It is worth referring back to that wheel diagram at the beginning of this part of the book. You might be keen to jump straight in with the "hows" but remember it is important to establish the *why* and *what* first in Steps 1 to 3 before you get to *how* in Step 4: Action.

When you carry out an inclusion survey, you will uncover all of these stories that you can use in your communication. When we carry out inclusion surveys, we hear all the horrible stories, but we also hear all the great stories. Sometimes when we share the stories of what people have actually done to help others and stop harassment or behaviours that are just not appropriate, we find that they are new to those in HR. When they read the stories in the qualitative part of the survey, they often become quite emotional.

Those are the stories that you want to tell internally whenever possible. I remember when we were analysing the financial sector, for all the bad stories we heard about how women and minorities were treated, we uncovered some great stories about how women and minorities actually got to the top and became role models for other underrepresented groups.

Take the same approach when you introduce new recruitment and promotion practices. Tell everybody about them, give examples to make everybody aware of why this is happening and also how they create great results.

Similarly, find stories of people who make the crossover to different silos. For instance, HR is often referred to as the "pink ghetto" because it is mainly women who work in these departments, while production tends to be male dominated. There are likely to be stories of men and women moving into departments that they would not traditionally be associated with. These are the stories you have to find and share.

Remember, this is a sprint – not a marathon. You want to move the needle fast.

There is a great example of this from the biggest company in Denmark, Maersk, which, in case you are not familiar with them, is a shipping company. Their HR department made a recruitment video targeting young talent in 2020, called "Together All the Way". It tells an engaging story about how trust transforms their industry, and the story is told by a rapper and people of all ethnicities dancing. The director of the video used to work there himself.

In Denmark, Maersk is seen as an old, traditional company that was founded by the great-grandfather of the current owner, and it has been a very strait-laced, blue collar and black suits, masculine company for a century. When Danes first saw that video, most of them thought, "That's not Maersk, they are just window dressing." However, now we know that Maersk has changed.

The company has a visionary new CEO and as a result of his efforts the culture is changing – and it is happening quickly. Their head of D&I is working miracles attracting young talent. When Maersk released that video, the company was hit by a shit storm in Danish media, and then the CEO, Soren Skou, came out and said, "Listen, I understand your reaction, you don't know that Maersk has changed, but what you're seeing in that video is how Maersk is today and that's how we are moving forward. This is also why last year was the best year ever at Maersk, despite the Coronavirus pandemic."[5]

---

[5]Friis, L. (2020), "Mærsk efter hård kritik af reklamevideo: »I Danmark er der enorme fordomme om, hvem vi er«", *Berlingske*, 18 November 2020, available at: https://www.berlingske.dk/virksomheder/maersk-efter-haard-kritik-af-reklamevideo-i-danmark-er-der-enorme.

This is how a CEO has to communicate. The CEO has to constantly back up what is happening on the journey towards a truly inclusive cultural transformation. Contrast that response from Maersk's CEO to how Google responded to Dr Gebru. Instead of firing her, they should have come out and supported the D&I agenda at the company.

How mature is your organisation in the area of diversity intelligence?

The table below comes from the book *Building an Inclusive Organization* by Stephen Frost and Raafi-Karim Alidina.[6] It sets out the typical maturity levels of organisations that have started working towards diversity and inclusion and shows how this evolves as the organisation develops its D&I maturity.

Table 4.1 Assessing organisational D&I maturity

Maturity	Diversity 1.0	Diversity 2.0	Inclusion 3.0
Meaning	Compliance-based to meet minimum criteria	Social responsibility and marketing-based	Embedded inclusion as a business strategy
Origins	Anti-discrimination, anti-harassment	Shareholder pressure	Recognition of unconscious bias and leadership deficits as a competitive disadvantage
Implementation	Compliance-based diversity training	Best-practice business case, diversity workshops	Targeted interventions and business case, transparency

---

[6]Alidina, R., and Frost, S. (2019), *Building an Inclusive Organization: Leveraging the Power of a Diverse Workforce*, Kogan Page.

Maturity	Diversity 1.0	Diversity 2.0	Inclusion 3.0
Leadership approach	Not involved	Voluntary ambassadors, unstructured commitment	Visible individual commitment and structured targets
Measurement	Legal reporting of cases	Demographic representation, attraction and retention, benchmarking	Yearly internal inclusion surveys, KPIs, attraction and retention
Accountability	Legal and HR	HR	C-suite

Summary

In this chapter, we have explored the different roles required to introduce and drive successful D&I initiatives within a company. We have looked at where different responsibilities lie and given an overview of some of the most important areas to focus on. We will cover inclusive leadership training and D&I Champions in greater detail in later chapters.

Firstly, however, we have to focus on the members of top management and synchronising them around the D&I agenda, because everything cascades down from here.

Chapter 5

Synchronising the Executive Team

Co-authored by Jens Rottbøll

Jens Rottbøll is Partner and Chief Consultant at the Living Institute. He has particular expertise in strategy and corporate values, company culture transformation, diversity intelligence and enhancing gender balance.

He has delivered remarkable results in his work, synchronising executive teams at organisations around the globe, helping them commit to the D&I agenda and find their voice. Jens is also one of just 10 certified LEGO® Serious Play® facilitator trainers in the world.

As we learned in the last chapter, for a D&I strategy to be effective it has to start at the top, and that means with the executive team. Within the executive team, everyone has to approach and support the D&I agenda with the same passion and drive. There is no room for people who only pay lip service to D&I. When we talk about synchronising the executive team, we mean aligning everyone behind the same goals and inspiring the same level of passion in all of them.

There are many areas where you need to synchronise your executive team and we will explore some of the most important from a diversity and inclusion perspective here.

Why is it so important for those in top management to be synchronised on D&I?

When an organisation starts working on D&I initiatives, it can be very easy to end up in muddy waters, even when you have the best of intentions. Instead of having clarity, you suddenly have confusion. There will always be groups of people within an organisation who are for or against an agenda for all kinds of reasons, some of which you will not even be able to imagine.

Imagine that the top management at an organisation has set out a D&I strategy and started to communicate it with others, but then they wade into these muddy waters. There are some board members, including the CEO, who are communicating with great passion, and others whose actions do not support what they are saying. At this point, people are likely to start questioning whether those in top management really mean what they are saying.

As soon as employees hear one person from top management saying something that is not aligned with the message that is coming from the CEO, they immediately lean back and say, "I knew it, they didn't mean it. It's just the flavour of the month."

It all comes back to the idea of accountability. Everybody in an organisation, whether they are for or against this change, is looking for gaps in accountability. Some people will be looking for those gaps to prove there is a divide in the top management team and others are looking at the situation and hoping that those in top management really mean what they are saying. This is what creates those muddy waters.

The concept of those within top management being synchronised on an issue is not rocket science. In fact, you will find it on the first page of any book about cultural transformation and crisis management. If you look at how many top management teams handle a crisis, they find it very easy to agree and say, "We'll go in this direction because of X, Y, Z." People lower down in the organisation also want to go in that direction because it saves jobs or even the company. In this situation, it is very easy to get everyone on the same page.

However, what is not yet fully understood by many top management teams is the importance of having this same synchronisation when it comes to D&I. Often when it comes to D&I, those in top management forget that they have to speak with one voice, tell the same stories and share the same narrative, otherwise there will be no impact.

When there is this lack of consistency, it becomes easy for others to challenge them and the direction they are trying to steer the company in, because people can point to different members of the team and say, "He said this, she's saying that, and you're saying the other."

In many cases, those in top management underestimate the need to be aligned when it comes to the field of D&I.

However, failing to create that alignment can ruin any D&I strategy within an organisation and, when this happens, we start to see the company wasting time and money. They try a number of different initiatives, but nobody believes in them and, as a result, people throughout the organisation check out. This is when an organisation can spend a lot of money and not see results.

Influences on CEOs and executive teams

Many CEOs and members of executive teams are influenced by factors they are probably not aware of when it comes to D&I.

Daughters influence a CEO's perception

For example, Henry Cronqvist, of Miami University,[1] studied Fortune 500 companies and found that male CEOs with daughters are shaped by them. This research revealed that companies run by CEOs with daughters are rated higher on the measures of diversity, employee relations and environmental stewardship than CEOs without daughters, and the CEOs with daughters also identified themselves more with women's preferences.

This was quantified through spending on the company's corporate social responsibility (CSR) programmes, with the average firm that is run by a CEO with a daughter spending 10.4% more of the firm's net income per year on CSR than the median company.

Imagine, then, that you have an executive team where some members have daughters and some do not. Those with daughters weigh the importance of inclusion and diversity differently to those without daughters. This means you would need to synchronise the executive team to speak with one voice whether they have daughters or not. This example highlights a perception gap.

In his book *A Promised Land*,[2] Barack Obama talks about how climate change is personal to him and he shares a story about a conversation he

---

[1]Cronqvist, H., and Yu, F. (2017), "Shaped by Their Daughters: Executives, Female Socialization, and Corporate Social Responsibility", September 3, 2017, *Journal of Financial Economics (JFE)*, available at: https://ssrn.com/abstract=2618358 or http://dx.doi.org/10.2139/ssrn.2618358.
[2]Obama, B. (2020), *A Promised Land*, Viking.

had over dinner with his family. His daughter Malia had written a report about tigers for school, describing how climate change and global warming is reducing the number of tigers living in the wild. She asked her father to do something about it and Obama explains that, after this conversation with Malia, he made climate change a greater priority in his presidency.

Female board members improve decision-making

There is a study showing that having female board members helps temper the overconfidence of a male CEO and improves overall decision-making for the company.[3] There are many examples in the corporate world where overconfident decisions have led to serious consequences for a business, from the collapse of Lehman Brothers during the 2008 financial crisis to the emissions cheating scandal at Volkswagen that I talked about in Chapter 1. You could argue that if there had been more women on the board in both those instances, those decisions would not have been taken.

This is exactly what Irene van Staveren investigated in her study,[4] "The Lehman Sisters hypothesis", discussing gender differences along three dimensions of financial behaviour: risk aversion and response to uncertainty, ethics and moral attitudes, and leadership.

If we think about top management as being both the board and the executive committee, there is a strong case that being more synchronised around the decisions they are making will lead to an improvement in bottom line results.

---

[3]Chen, J., Goergen, M., Leung, W.S., and Song, W. (2019), "Research: When Women Are on Boards, Male CEOs Are Less Overconfident", *Harvard Business Review*, 12 September 2019, available at: https://hbr.org/2019/09/research-when-women-are-on-boards-male-ceos-are-less-overconfident.

[4]van Staveren, I. (2014), "The Lehman Sisters Hypothesis", *Cambridge Journal of Economics*, Volume 38 (Issue 5), 995–1014, available at: https://doi.org/10.1093/cje/beu010.

Why is D&I strategy different to other corporate strategies?

What is interesting is that you rarely see the same kinds of problems when businesses are rolling out other corporate strategies. In our experience, it is because traditional corporate strategy work involves a more rational process with fewer feelings involved.

On the surface at least, corporate strategy is a more rational process that centres around your customers, your processes, your competencies and so on. These are areas that those in top management typically feel comfortable with.

However, when it comes to creating a D&I strategy and synchronising top management around that strategy, we often find that top management do not know what they really know. They feel uncertain in this field. They have a lot of feelings and attitudes. Some of them may have read around the subject and feel positive about the agenda. Some may even understand the business case.

This is all on a conscious level, and what we need to do in order to synchronise top management is take them beneath this conscious level to their unconscious knowledge. We also have to help them tap into their feelings, because this is what makes them trustworthy to others when they speak about this agenda.

Why is D&I different?

The process of accessing this unconscious knowledge and creating synchronisation within top management takes more than a PowerPoint presentation or an exercise with Post-It notes. What you need is a tool that, similar to LEGO® Serious Play® (which I will discuss below), can tap into the subconscious, feelings and tacit implicit knowledge of those in top management to create that synchronisation.

As already said, the field of D&I is different to the other areas associated with running a business. For many in top management positions, this is an unknown field, which is why they need some help to develop their D&I vision, while knowing and respecting the existing culture.

What we see time and again is those in top management deciding to introduce a D&I initiative and saying, "We want this. It's a great idea. Go and do it." They believe this is enough and that they can leave it to somebody else to "go and do it". However, in doing so they underestimate the process and doom it to failure by leaving somebody else to implement it. This is despite knowing, intellectually, that it is a good idea for the whole management team to be synchronised on the issue.

When you think about it from a business perspective, you would not imagine being unsynchronised within the top team when it comes to other areas of business strategy. The difference with D&I, as we have said, is that it is not an area that many business people feel comfortable in.

If a company decided to expand into China, for example, those in top management would know that they needed to do this, this and this, because they are excellent business people and they feel at home in these areas.

D&I is different. It often feels as though you are talking about something fluffy. There are a lot of feelings involved, as well as a lot of resistance. Within a board, there may be some people who are very passionate about the agenda and others who are very hopeful this will pass soon. This lack of synchronisation is what creates those muddy waters and that will, in turn, prevent D&I initiatives from succeeding.

Having this synchronisation of top management is a make or break factor in the D&I journey of a company.

What do you have to invest to synchronise your top management team?

If we look at this from a highly practical perspective, the minimum effort is to invest in a one- to two-day workshop to get the management team aligned. When you look at the return on investment on just that workshop, it is enormous.

To achieve these results, we at the Living Institute use the LEGO® Serious Play® methodology. In our experience, when a top management team uses this tool for one or two days, they save about six months of time and they develop a strong shared narrative around what they are doing in the field of D&I. That saves the businesses we work with a lot of money further down the road, because people trust what they say, not to mention significantly accelerating the progress with their D&I agenda.

Who do you involve?

For a session such as this, ideally you will include the executive committee and the board, because they are generally just as unsure as the executive committee about how to create and run D&I initiatives that get results.

What is LEGO® Serious Play®?

This is a very simple tool where you use your hands to build LEGO® models. Using your hands allows you to change behavioural thinking, because when you use your hands to create something, that rebuilds your brain. This is how we enable people to tap into their unconscious knowledge of the D&I agenda.

At the Living Institute, LEGO® Serious Play® is our preferred tool, but the point is that you need a specific tool to accelerate the process. Otherwise it typically takes the executive committee six months to a year to get their stomachs, hearts and heads around it and put all of these things together.

Although LEGO® Serious Play® was not created specifically for D&I strategy, we have found that it is a particularly effective tool in this field. This is because it links back to the concept of clearing the muddy waters that often manifest around D&I initiatives, and using this tool helps any executive committee to navigate all the different feelings, expectations and agendas within society that typically make developing an effective D&I strategy challenging.

Why does this process work?

One of the ways in which this process is so impactful is through different people within the group sharing stories in a safe space.

When we create this environment, we find men and women will share stories that they would not normally be comfortable sharing in a typical meeting, because they all feel that this is a safe space. It is these stories that impact people.

Each of the stories that people share contributes to a stronger understanding of the actual issues people are facing. Throughout these sessions, we often hear people making statements like, "Oh, I didn't know you were so impacted by these things" and "I have never heard about this in that area of our company" and "Why didn't anybody tell me? If they'd told me about that I would have done something", and so on.

These are what we refer to as "small ah-ha moments". It is often difficult to find those by following a standard consultancy process.

The process we use with LEGO® Serious Play® enables participants to be more themselves and more authentic than simply their role within the company. It cuts through both the formal and informal hierarchies and it cuts through roles and responsibilities by creating this safe space where people can collate how they really see things from their own point of view.

For many top managers, having this time and space to think freely about an issue is a rarity. They are paid millions to make quick decisions, to provide quick answers and to get things done. It is not often that they have time to really unpick something so complex.

Death by 1,000 cuts

During one LEGO® Serious Play® session we ran one model particularly stood out, not only for those involved in the session but also for us as consultants. One woman in the group had made a simple LEGO® model, with one LEGO® minifigure holding a sword standing at the centre.

Figure 5.1 Death by a thousand cuts – built by a participant in a LEGO® Serious Play® strategy session

When it was her turn to share the story of her model, she said the following:

"There are a lot of good people in this company and they don't have bad intentions. There is a policy that says there should be women in top management, and we have policies for equal pay and everything like that. But what kills me are the 1,000 cuts I experience every day.

These are just small things that kill me by 1,000 cuts every day; it might be being ignored in a meeting, being told to be quiet because you're a woman; seeing other people get promoted without the right competencies and being overlooked for promotion yourself. These are the 1,000 cuts that are killing me."

That story impacted everybody in the room, because they had never seen it like that. In 30 seconds she explained something that nobody else had experienced, and they felt it and for a moment they were in her shoes. That is how you change a culture.

It is so easy to rely on the fact that you have policies at your company and you may even have a head of D&I. You have what, on the outside, looks like a nice package, but it is not real.

This process is a way to find a shared understanding of the brutal reality of the situation that these companies have to navigate. It is a powerful way to help the members of top management understand a situation that they rarely get to see first-hand.

This also demonstrates why it is vital for top management to be synchronised and shows why you need an unorthodox and powerful tool to achieve that alignment. When people feel it in their stomach and start understanding the complexity of what is going on, they realise that policies and good intentions on their own are not enough.

Strong facilitation is essential for effective sessions

As the aim of these sessions is to create a safe space where everyone involved feels free to talk, you need to have strong facilitators. It is important to cut through any power differentials in the room to make sure that everybody participating has an equal voice.

This is how and why these sessions work – they are about getting everybody's voices out in the open, putting everyone's thoughts, experiences and feelings on the table and creating a synchronised story based on them.

An overview of a LEGO® Serious Play® session

When we run a one-day workshop with a client, we begin by sharing the agenda for the day and explain that we are going to use LEGO® as part of the play process. Some people get excited, others are afraid and some just feel that it is silly and a waste of time.

Having mixed feelings among the participants is common, so we teach everyone how to use the methodology and usually spend about one hour warming up, so that everyone feels safe. After this, we move into the stage of the workshop where that model I described above, about the 1,000 cuts, came up.

Everybody has LEGO® in front of them and is going to use this to build a small model that tells a story. This model can be abstract, concrete or metaphorical – which one does not matter. The question I asked in the session where the model of 1,000 cuts was created was, "What is the core density of the culture at this company when it comes to diversity and inclusion?" I told them to be brutally honest about what it looks and feels like.

Each person then builds their own model that tells a small story about what they have experienced and what they see around them.

This process has to take a very inward focus. Everyone has to forget about clients, the future and everything else. It is all about themselves and the company.

The model of 1,000 cuts was just one of 25 that were built in that session. That model was one truth, but there were 24 other truths around the table. Other people had a different opinion. For instance, one white man said that since the company had introduced its D&I agenda, it had created a blame culture and, as a white man, he felt terrible and did not enjoy going to work any more.

Both of these models, although very different, are correct. They are right for both of these people. These truths co-exist. The reason why this session is so transformative is that this is often the first time that people have reached a point where they are able to express, share or understand other people's perspectives.

When there are 25 models in a room, of course a lot of stories overlap, but there are always nuances and differences between them.

Based on these individual models, the next step is to build a shared model. When there are 25 people, we would split them into two groups and ask each one to work together to build a shared model of how they see the world right now. We want them to be brutally honest about their reality.

This model will be much deeper, much better and much more nuanced than any of the individual models alone. This is a representation of collective intelligence. How does this tie in with synchronisation? Imagine that all 12 people in that group can look at one shared model and say, "Yes, that's how it is." That is synchronisation and those 12 people now all share the same story.

When we have this alignment we can move forward. The next step is to duplicate the process by asking each individual to build a model showing what they want the company to look like in two years' time. Each person shares their model and, once again in groups, they build a shared model showing what they want the company to look like in two years' time. Using this collective intelligence, we arrive at a shared story about how the future will look.

This process leads to synchronised teams because you end up with one model that everybody understands. They have all contributed to that model and therefore each person owns that model.

It is a way of bringing everybody's truths together and helping everybody understand one another. This is particularly important in our VUCA world and especially within the field of D&I, which is so complex. Our truths all co-exist and if top management does not understand that, they tend to forget the truth that is not closest to them.

The power of synchronising top management using this process is not only that everyone shares the same story, but everyone understands *why* they have this story. The LEGO® Serious Play® process is also a literal demonstration of inclusivity.

Connecting the two models

Once we have these two shared models – one showing how the company is now and one showing how they want it to be in two years' time – the next step is to work out how you connect them.

Imagine that the model of where you are now is at one end of the table, and the model of where you want to be in two years is at the other. Between them is just empty space. The logical step is to decide what initiatives you need to introduce to go from one to the other.

Once again, we follow the process of each person building an individual model of an initiative and then working to align everyone around the shared models that go into the centre of the table to bridge that gap. As well as agreeing on which models you want to use, it is also essential that you decide which models you want to look at first.

During this step, you build out the roles and responsibilities that are needed to make this happen. When you are doing this exercise to synchronise top management, this process involves knowing what those in management need to do and what their roles are, as well as what roles others in the organisation will play.

This is when you can move on to thinking about the creation of your task force, what initiatives you will introduce, what order you will introduce them in and how you will monitor them.

There is a great deal of power in these 3D models. Often what we say simply disappears. The words we use, unless someone captures them, are said and then they are gone. When there is a 3D model it is there for everyone to see. The companies we work with keep their models, which act as a reminder that there might be this woman who is suffering 1,000 cuts every day from a sword wielded by others, for instance. This man with the sword does not go away until someone takes him away because the cultural transformation succeeded and what he symbolised no longer exists.

Can't we just look at the data?

As I mentioned earlier in the book, we carry out inclusion surveys for the companies that we work with at the Living Institute to uncover all of these stories. However, when it comes to synchronising the top management team, it is important that we do not start with this data.

The reason is that if you only use data, it becomes an intellectual process, rather than one that gets into people's subconscious level. The people who work in top management positions are really good at absorbing data and information, but when it is presented in this form, it does not encourage them to share their own deeper insights or tap into their subconscious.

When we run workshops to synchronise top management, we often have the data from our inclusion survey, but we choose to hold this back until they have had the opportunity to create their own narrative. We want them to be able to say, "This is what it looks like at our company. This is our culture. This is how we want it to be in the future."

It is a basic strategic concept, defining where you are now and where you want to be. Once the top management team has defined this, then we share the data from the inclusion survey with them.

When we do this, we ask them to look for any differences between what they see in the survey and the data they shared among themselves during the session. What is interesting is that they trust the data we show them because it is usually 80–90% aligned with what they have already shared.

The reason this is so powerful is that it shows the executive committee that, if they take action in this area, they are aligned with what other people at their organisation expect and already see within the organisation.

At this point, the executive committee can recognise that everyone in the organisation can see the same challenges and that many want to go to some of the same places, which gives them confidence in the D&I strategy they then create.

Data is certainly important, and I will talk more about this in Chapter 6, but when it comes to creating that essential synchronisation in top management, the focus is on the deeper insights they can share, their subconscious and their feelings, as well as the intellectual process associated with analysing the data.

Why does this method work so well in D&I?

In 2013/14, we went through this process with a new logistics team from the Danish Army to synchronise their operations before they were sent to Afghanistan. This particular story does not fall under the scope of D&I, but it illustrates why LEGO® Serious Play® often works in a D&I setting.

They carried out the session in Denmark, but when they went to Afghanistan they took the LEGO® Serious Play® model they created with them and made it the centrepiece of the commander's office. Every time something changed, they changed the model accordingly.

Therefore, if there had been a little guy with a sword in their model, they would have removed him when they could see he was not a problem any more, and so on.

To bring this back to D&I, you can use annual inclusion surveys at your organisation to do exactly the same thing. If, the year after you make this model, you do not hear stories about people suffering 1,000 cuts, you can take that man with the sword out, because you have addressed the issue and solved it by introducing the right initiatives.

Your model is dynamic and can evolve as your organisation changes, so that the parts of the model that are no longer relevant can disappear as you solve issues.

These models allow you to communicate clearly around your agenda, which is particularly important in the field of D&I. Going back to the Danish logistics team in Afghanistan, they used their LEGO® model to communicate with the US and UK forces they were working with.

The team took the UK chief in command and the US chief in command into their tent, showed them their model and explained how they saw the situation and what they needed from each side, all in 3D. They shared how they would support the UK and US troops and they explained their targets and the challenges they were facing from a logistics perspective.

Afterwards, the UK and US chiefs in command came to the Danish tent with their own small LEGO® figures and asked for them to be part of the Danish model. You cannot achieve this level of buy-in through PowerPoint.

Summary

In this chapter, we have explained in detail why synchronising top management teams is vital if you want to succeed.

LEGO® Serious Play® is a powerful tool for creating deep synchronisation within top management and for communicating the situation as it is – the vision, the challenges and the initiatives – to the rest of the organisation.

If you are still in doubt as to the validity of LEGO® Serious Play®, I will leave you with one final thought. Words can never be as clear as models and that is why models are such an old strategic tool. Even though Napoleon would not have used LEGO® to plan his battles, he certainly had many little figures with swords in their hands.

This visual and 3D aspect of models makes everything clear to everyone, and it is the core reason why people have been using them for hundreds of years.

Chapter 6

Basing Your D&I Strategies on Data

Diversity intelligence has to be driven by data

As already mentioned, there has been no significant progress within the diversity and inclusion agenda for many years in practically all sectors and industries globally. One of the things we have recently learned is the importance of a data-driven approach to D&I strategies.

If the inclusion survey had not uncovered this immense perception gap between top management and the rest of the organisation, they would not have had this notable wake-up call.

Without this data, organisations build their activities on a very subjective foundation consisting of guesswork, myths and anecdotes, where, depending on your personal identity and background, you will have a specific viewpoint on what diversity and inclusion is, to what extent it matters and how it matters.

Uncovering the real story

To strengthen inclusion, a multi-national energy company contracted the Living Institute to conduct an in-depth inclusion survey collecting both quantitative and qualitative data. Of particular interest to the leadership team was attracting and retaining young talent.

However, when results came in from their global offices, we could see that there was a concern among senior employees who had been with the company for many years. Given the corporate emphasis on creating an attractive environment for young people, the leadership team had forgotten the older generations.

In fact, we could show them that their more senior employees who had been with the company for many years were statistically more likely to feel excluded as a result of not feeling they belonged in the new company culture. The leaders realised that they were at risk of losing hundreds of years of combined experience and expertise if they did not design a system in which their senior employees could thrive as well.

This also highlights one of the biggest mistakes top management teams can make, which is to base their D&I initiatives on current trends and best practices without a clear, data-driven understanding of their own culture.

As we have already discussed, diversity is anything that makes us different from each other, which means there are many different perceptions, approaches and ways to talk about and deal with inclusion and diversity.

At the Living Institute, one of the most important things we have learned from our clients is that there is a need to hold this conversation in a shared and common language, identifying common challenges as well as common opportunities.

The conversation needs to be about not what diversity and inclusion give us, but about what homogeneity and exclusion take away from us, and even how dangerous they can be for the survival of a business.

The only way to start this meaningful conversation and ensure everyone is talking about the same reality is to take a data-driven approach, using objective and statistically significant facts. In doing so, everybody is able to participate and we are able to understand how we differ from each other, as well as see things from a different perspective.

What is an inclusion survey?

An inclusion survey is essentially a perception gap analysis, which shows the level of inclusion that different identity groups within your company experience and how they thrive differently in this culture. Through an inclusion survey, you find the gaps and then use your D&I strategy to close them.

The inclusion surveys that we carry out have three elements: a diagnosis, a compass and an analysis of the company's culture. The data from an inclusion survey can help your organisation to course correct or recalibrate the trajectory of your D&I journey.

For example, a company might be travelling in one direction, but when we carry out the inclusion survey we find that this course was guided by myths and stereotypical thinking. The data we provide shows which direction they need to move in to deal with the business-critical challenges they actually face.

This survey often shows why none of the initiatives the company has previously implemented have worked, because the issues often lie in different places than they thought.

For instance, the story I shared at the beginning of the chapter revealed that it was the older, rather than the younger, generations who were feeling excluded. Without that knowledge, that company would likely have continued on its current path, potentially losing decades of valuable experience along the way.

The DNA of an inclusion survey

Our inclusion surveys include three elements:

- An online questionnaire (quantitative).
- Interviews (qualitative).
- Focus groups (qualitative).

There are four main areas of focus within the survey:

- Belonging, wellbeing and psychological safety.
- Level of inclusion.
- Engagement level.
- How long respondents will stay at the company (staff turnover).

The key to finding significant and valid perception gaps is to segment the respondents correctly and to cross-tabulate the responses to find the perception gap between the different identity groups at different levels in the organisation.

We recommend that our clients carry out annual inclusion surveys in much the same way as annual employee engagement surveys.

However, the two surveys serve two different functions. Gathering the inclusion data on an annual basis allows you to adjust your initiatives to secure maximum effect and is crucial in order to win the sprint and avoid the decade-long marathons.

"At LEGO we have an inclusion index, which is made up of a series of questions around sense of belonging, feeling appreciated, safe to share views and opinions. We measure and track and we set targets. And then, of course, we have all kinds of metrics associated with them."
– Loren I. Shuster, Chief People Officer & Head of Corporate Affairs, The LEGO Group

The main purposes of an inclusion survey

There are two main purposes to an inclusion survey. The first is that it allows us to open our eyes to what diversity means to us, as well as to what it means to our colleagues, and how this impacts our view of the world.

This understanding and knowledge is a productive conversation starter. It helps everyone start talking about diversity and inclusion as something within the company and between the people we work with every day, rather than as an abstract concept that some are passionate about and some are not.

The second purpose of an inclusion survey is to give us a clearer picture of what the challenges are. We know that there has not been much progress in the area of diversity and inclusion in many companies around the world, and the data from this survey uncovers why.

Often when we speak to companies before they have carried out an inclusion survey, they think they know why their previous initiatives have not worked. They are fairly sure they know what the problems are and where the challenges lie. However, once we carry out an inclusion survey these businesses realise they were not even close to guessing what the true problems were. These surveys are a key turning point for the majority of the organisations we work with at the Living Institute.

What businesses often discover is that they had mistaken myths and stereotypes for the truth. We all have narratives and stories about minorities, majorities and diversity, but when we compare these narratives and stories to the facts and data from an inclusion survey, we often find that the truth lies elsewhere. However, many D&I initiatives are still based on myths and guesswork rather than facts and data, despite the negative consequences this brings.

Examples of myths we have encountered

- Women are not ambitious.
- We only look for competencies when we hire.
- There is not enough minority talent in the organisation.
- Family life is the primary reason for women's lack of ambitions and career opportunities.
- There are equal opportunities for men and women and minority groups.

All of these myths have been proven wrong in studies, research and our own inclusion surveys.

As an example, in one recent inclusion survey we conducted, 27% of women disagreed that men and women had equal opportunities, as did 13% of men. In the same company, there are equal numbers of men and women at entry level, yet no women in the executive team. This is a typical example of privilege blindness.

How myths lead to the wrong initiatives

Myths invariably lead to companies introducing the wrong D&I initiatives. In many cases, not only do these initiatives not have a positive effect on diversity and inclusion, but they actually harm progress in this area.

For example, that women are not ambitious is a tenacious myth we often come across in companies all over the world. It is also a myth that a lot of companies have reacted to this by introducing leadership training programmes for their female talent, hoping to make women more ambitious and therefore lead to more women reaching top management.

"It's difficult to know if she has the ambition to become a leader. I haven't asked her."

– Male respondent to an inclusion survey

One of my colleagues was recently on the radio talking about unconscious bias training, why it works and why there are so few women in leadership positions. One male listener sent a text message to the show stating that the reason for this was "pure mathematics".

His contention, and the myth that he believed to be true, was that there is a larger pool of men who want leadership positions compared to women and, therefore, it is to be expected that there are more men than women in leadership positions.

In fact, the reality revealed over and over again in our inclusion surveys, as well as other research like a 2017 study from the Boston Consulting Group,[1] is that women are already more ambitious than their male colleagues and this idea that they do not want leadership positions simply is not true.

At the Living Institute, we conducted an inclusion survey for seven institutions in the financial sector in 2019. We asked respondents to score themselves on a scale from 1 to 10 on whether they had ambitions to become a leader or remain in leadership by moving to a higher level.

Female respondents scored themselves an average of 8.5 out of 10 on this scale, compared to male respondents who scored themselves an average of 7.6 out of 10. **This data shows that women are more, not less, ambitious than their male colleagues.**

When we looked specifically at the responses from women at the highest levels of leadership within these organisations, their score jumped to

---

[1]Krentz, M., Tracey, C., and Tsusaka, M. (2017), "Dispelling the Myths of the Gender 'Ambition Gap'", Boston Consulting Group, April 5, 2017, available at: https://www.bcg.com/publications/2017/people-organization-leadership-change-dispelling-the-myths-of-the-gender-ambition-gap.

9.7 out of 10, again above their male colleagues who scored themselves 8.8 out of 10.

The real reason why women had not reached top positions in this sector was also revealed through this survey.

60% of the female leaders at the organisations believed there was enough female leadership talent already at their companies, compared to just 20% of male leaders. In other words, female leaders could see the talented women whereas the male leaders couldn't see the talent standing in front of them, unless that talent was a man.

The data demonstrated that male leaders exhibited an unconscious bias against female leadership talent, which was the real reason why more women had not advanced to higher leadership positions.

In this example, the right solution would be to introduce inclusive leadership training with elements of unconscious bias training and tools to sponsor and manage women and men equally.

The main learning outcome from this inclusion survey was that if companies base their actions on the myth that women are not ambitious, they will waste money on "fixing" women by providing female leadership training. Instead, to see real change, they need to focus on mobilising men and offering inclusive leadership training.

Also, by introducing initiatives such as female leadership training programmes, an organisation tells its people two things: firstly, that they have to do this because women are not as ambitious as men and, secondly, that women are not as competent as men because they need extra training that men do not need.

Both of those beliefs are, according to the data, incorrect and therefore taking this action is counterproductive.

"There is a long way to go for female employees. Only a few reach senior manager level. It is shameful that we don't have more women on top levels. I could understand if we don't have the talent in the pool, but we have fabulous women in our company. I have worked with them but their competencies are not being recognised. We have lost good women because of a lack of opportunities."
— Male specialist in the energy sector inclusion survey 2020

The positive side effects of carrying out regular inclusion surveys

There are two main side effects of conducting regular inclusion surveys within an organisation.

The first is that, in doing so, you are sending a clear signal to everyone in your organisation that you mean what you say about D&I. You are asking for help to make your company a great place to work for everyone and the survey kick-starts the dialogue. By virtue of simply asking these questions, you are mobilising a lot of people behind the agenda, regardless of the answers you receive.

I still remember the interview, which I quoted from earlier, with the male respondent who expressed how happy he was when he got the link to the inclusion survey in his mailbox – it gave him the feeling that things were going to change now, he said.

Secondly, when you have the data from within your own organisation, it is no longer possible for anyone to deny that there is a problem. There are often pockets of resistance to the inclusion of diversity, and in many cases this resistance is subtle or even subconscious. However, when you have data that has come not from some abstract source but the people standing next to you, it encourages everyone to take action.

For example, the facts and figures might tell you that every second woman you hire will leave your company within the first two years of her tenure. In addition, this data will show you that 20% of the men who work for you intend to leave the company because women do not have equal opportunities.

This reveals something important about the company's culture. These men who say they want to leave are not only driven by the lack of equal opportunities, but by the broader culture within the company. A lack of equal opportunities is just one way that this negative company culture manifests. These people are actively looking to leave the company because the culture feels unbearable to them.

For top management teams in particular, being confronted with these hard facts and figures often shows them that they have been tone deaf or have overlooked an issue. Think back to the example I shared at the beginning of the chapter, about the company where its older employees no longer felt they belonged. This was an issue that those in top management were previously unaware of.

Why are inclusion surveys foundational?

There is no other serious aspect of business that would be approached with the guesswork and lack of concrete data that is used to justify different diversity and inclusion initiatives. Carrying out inclusion surveys is essential to ensure that D&I initiatives are introduced with certainty that they will work, rather than a process of trial and error.

If you keep approaching the D&I agenda at your organisation by relying on the narratives you tell yourself, the myths you believe and guesswork about where the problems lie, you will never introduce initiatives that make a difference because you will never get to the root cause of why you have problems in the first place.

Another reason why conducting inclusion surveys is so important for D&I agendas is that the results that come out of these surveys show those in top management that they need to allocate a budget to make changes. This budget needs to be determined based on the data and strategic initiatives that need to be put in place.

When we looked at all of the clients we had at the Living Institute at the start of 2021, we could see that it was the HR director or manager who had approached us from every company we were working with. In nine out of 10 cases, this HR manager did not have a budget and therefore had to fight for money for every workshop or initiative.

Given the business-critical nature of D&I, more companies need to allocate appropriate budgets to it, but all too often they are failing to provide even a fraction of the financial support necessary. Making a cultural transformation is costly, but the good news is that it has a tenfold return on investment.

It is, however, financially wise for a business to wait until it has the results of its inclusion survey before allocating money to D&I initiatives, because this survey provides a very clear indication of where to spend money to have the greatest impact.

Shining the light on blindspots

There was one story that particularly struck me from the survey we carried out across the organisations in the financial sector.

After we have carried out the quantitative analysis and interviews as part of an inclusion survey, we also conducted focus groups. These are always held with members of top management after the survey has been completed and are an opportunity to present our findings and ask what surprises them about the results.

When we were holding a focus group with one of the companies in the financial sector, the CEO arrived 10 minutes late and, as he entered the room, stated, "Now we're going to hear how sexist we all are."

When we reached the figures that I shared above, about how 60% of female managers believed there was enough female leadership talent already in the organisation, compared to just 20% of male leaders, this CEO became rather upset. His response to this data was, "How come women can see this talent and I can't?" It was a wake-up call for him, because the data was indisputable and showed why so many women had left the company.

In this instance, the CEO instantly said that they needed to act now and immediately allocated a budget, because they had visibility about what they needed to act upon. By shining a light on this blindspot, the CEO and other members of top management were not only able to take action, but also had the desire to allocate a budget to improving the situation.

Summary

I have said from the beginning of this book that data is important when you are making decisions about the D&I agenda at any organisation, and now I have shared how you can collect data that will help to uncover your blindspots, myths and perception gaps that need immediate action and steer your company in the right direction on its diversity intelligence journey.

As well as ensuring that any initiatives you introduce have greater impact, basing these decisions on data will also save you money. You will make progress on your D&I agenda, you will be better placed to tackle those pockets of resistance and get buy-in from everyone across the business, and you will see a return on the investment you put into your D&I initiatives. Most importantly, however, you are telling the organisation and everyone who works there that you care.

This is the power that data has for driving your D&I agenda forward. In the next chapter, we are going to explore inclusive leadership training and why this is such a useful tool.

Chapter 7

Inclusive Leadership Training
Co-authored by Kasper Jelsbech Knudsen

Kasper Jelsbech Knudsen is a Chief Consultant at the Living Institute. He holds a PhD in Anthropology and is a brilliant diversity strategist and keynote speaker. He specialises in inclusive leadership, advancing gender parity, unconscious bias mitigation and cross-culture, as well as cross-disciplinary, collaborations.

Kasper has helped many multi-national organisations enhance their diversity intelligence. He is also a LEGO® Serious Play® facilitator and certified provider of the individual assessment tool: Intercultural Readiness Check.

What is inclusive leadership and why should we care?

Inclusive leadership is, in essence, engaging leadership around an inspirational D&I strategy. Why is it important that you care whether the leaders in your business are inclusive or not? As we learned in Chapter 2, diversity alone will not bring anything valuable to the company; in fact, it is likely to do the opposite.

Highlighting the need for inclusive leadership – Part 1

Imagine you are part of an organisation with a global presence and a high degree of diversity in the workforce across all areas, from age, ethnicity and gender to nationality, sexual orientation and faith. Imagine also that 80% of the leaders and managers in this organisation are *not* practising inclusive leadership.

In fact they are practising the opposite. They are unaware of this and it is certainly not intentional. With everything happening in the world to create uncertainty at the moment, including the Covid-19 pandemic, these managers are struggling to navigate the complexity, diversity and their own role in this ever-changing environment.

Now, I would like you to imagine an inclusion survey that measures the level of inclusion and belonging at this company. What would that show? I will come back to this at the end of the chapter.

Without inclusion, an inclusive process and inclusive leadership, diversity actually damages business performance. In fact, we know from research that if you have diverse teams without inclusive leadership, these teams will probably perform worse than most other teams. Remember the bell curve graphs from Chapter 2, which show that diversity without inclusion has a negative impact?

Further evidence of the importance of inclusive leadership when managing diversity comes from research conducted by Deloitte.[1] It found that whether or not people feel included in a team is up to the leader (both senior executives and managers) 70% of the time. This effect is even stronger among minority groups.

---

[1]Bourke, J., and Dillon, B. (January 2018), *The Diversity and Inclusion Revolution*, Deloitte, available at: https://www2.deloitte.com/content/dam/insights/us/articles/4209_Diversity-and-inclusion-revolution/DI_Diversity-and-inclusion-revolution.pdf.

What is more, an increase in individuals' feelings of inclusion translates to a 17% increase in perceived team performance, a 20% improvement in decision-making quality and a 29% improvement in collaboration.

Although inclusive leadership is important, it is not the only factor at play. There also needs to be a process that disrupts our human tendency to always look for sameness in others. This tendency causes us to avoid diversity or differences when we encounter them.

As an example, I am sure you have had a conversation with someone different from you where you felt as though the person you were speaking to just did not seem to understand what you were communicating to them. You could both feel this miscommunication happening and it created an awkward, uncomfortable feeling. These feelings of discomfort then cause you to avoid each other. However, the reason this miscommunication happened in the first place is down to diversity.

Diversity can cause friction, and many people find it difficult to integrate things they are not used to. As I touched upon in Chapter 4, this results in cocooning, where leaders surround themselves with people like themselves.

Therefore, to advance diversity, all leaders need to become inclusive leaders and, more importantly, all leaders *can* become inclusive leaders.

Where are you on the inclusivity spectrum?

The following is a simple exercise that we ask participants to complete during our workshops. It is designed to open your awareness to any cocooning tendencies you might have and to help you begin to understand where your blindspots are.

Exercise

Make a list of the 10 people you interact with on a daily basis in your leadership role. These could be direct reports or others within the organisation.

Once you have that list, highlight the names of the people who you give the most resources to, the ones you spend the most time with, the ones you joke with and the ones you have lunch with. Now that you have highlighted your list, reflect on how similar those people you have just highlighted are to you. They might be similar in gender, age, educational background or maybe even in opinions and attitude.

If you find that these people, we will call them your proteges, are completely different to you, that indicates that you are a person who seeks out diversity, which is, of course, a key trait of an inclusive leader. However, if you find that your proteges are very similar to you, it indicates you are working more towards the exclusive leadership end of the spectrum.

The next step, regardless of where you fall on the spectrum, is to consider whether there is anyone on that list whom you might have overlooked.

What is interesting is that, often when we carry out this exercise, leaders tell us that the reason they overlook certain people is because they are "difficult". In a global setting it might be that their English is not very good or it could be that they always ask counter questions and delay meetings. Maybe they are introverted and do not speak up.

Why is that interesting? Because what makes people "difficult" in the eyes of the leader is that they are different to them. The leader finds it hard to see something they can mirror him or herself in, and that means the leader overlooks them.

This exercise is a good way to not only explore what you look for in your proteges as a leader, but also to understand to what degree you create "in groups" and "out groups". It is an opportunity to ask yourself what you overlook and what you might miss in terms of diversity.

Having self-awareness is important if you are to make a change in how you lead.

"The men would form a circle that didn't let me in. It wasn't natural for them to invite me in. I decided to buy high-heeled shoes to be taller than them and thus get their attention. The non-verbal and apparently unimportant actions and gestures actually mean a lot."
– Female leader and respondent to an inclusion survey

What characterises a successful inclusive leader?

Interestingly, a lot of the inclusive leaders we have met through the Living Institute do not talk about inclusion or describe themselves as inclusive. Being inclusive is simply something that they are. However, they do talk about the need to act with empathy towards others, to listen to other people's input and to be aware of their blindspots when making decisions.

We have found that the main and most important characteristic of an inclusive leader is that they are diversity intelligent. This means having humility, empathy, cultural intelligence, gender intelligence and generational intelligence, as well as being a conscious leader and being conscious in every area of their life.

In short, having these traits means you are accepting that, as human beings, we are different in all kinds of ways. When you think like this, you are not only looking at how you can bridge those differences in an inclusive way, but also how you can celebrate those differences and unleash potential. This is diversity intelligence.

By exploring each of the traits that make up diversity intelligence through the lens of inclusive leadership, we can see why each is essential for any inclusive leader.

Humility

Are you humble enough to know that you yourself are susceptible to biases that can cloud your decision-making in your everyday work? This ties into the leadership philosophy that is sometimes associated with Steve Jobs and others like him, in that you hire people who are smarter than you or who have a different perspective to you, you know you do not know everything and you are aware you do not need to be the smartest or strongest in the group to be a respected leader.

Steve Jobs is actually an interesting leader to look at, because he was great at managing diversity within his teams and businesses and at unleashing potential, but he was not always a pleasant person to be around and was known for losing his temper. In fact, this goes to show that you can lack other core leadership traits and still create a highly successful company if you are able to manage diversity well and harness that potential.

The old paradigm was that you had to be the smartest person or the most qualified person in the room to be a good leader, but today this is not the case. You are there to facilitate the talent and potential of others.

It is just as important that you are able to listen to others' perspectives because this allows you to develop a sense and awareness of your own blindspots. Being humble is one of the key traits of an inclusive leader.

Empathy

Are you able to put yourself in other people's shoes, to understand their needs and perspectives? An inclusive leader is able to empathise on an individual level but, perhaps more importantly, they are also able to create empathy among all the members of a team.

If everyone on a team is empathetic, inclusion will skyrocket. The team will be diversity intelligent. As a leader, you need to take responsibility for creating a culture of empathy within your team.

This means being able to develop empathy for people who are different to you. If you only empathise with those who are similar to you, you are creating that cocoon I talked about in Chapter 4. Instead, you have to empathise with people who are a different age, a different gender, a different nationality, from a different cultural or ethnic background, and who have radically different life experiences to you.

Being able to empathise in this way is not possible without diversity intelligence. Unconsciously, we mirror ourselves in other people and take our experiences and project them on to others. To develop empathy, we almost look for sameness, which is where the challenge lies.

However, it is important that we become aware of this unconscious tendency and always remember that we mirror ourselves in others and project our own life stories on to them. It can be very easy to think, "If I have experienced this then you have too", but this is not necessarily the case. This is why you have to become aware of that unconscious tendency and look for it in all your interactions.

The art of being an empathetic leader is in feeling empathy for people who are radically different to you, not only feeling empathy for people who are like you. However, empathy stems from a feeling of sameness, which of course will not help a leader of diverse teams who wants to nurture diversity of thought. This means empathy is not a given in a diverse setting.

You have to become aware of this paradox and stubbornly train your empathy muscle for people who are radically different from you. This is harder to achieve than you might think, because it is typically an unconscious process and you have to train your empathy muscle to relate to the invisible differences between us as much as to the visible ones.

Cultural intelligence

As a leader, what do you need to know about different nationalities in order to act with intelligence towards them? For example, as a Japanese leader this could mean thinking about how to approach working with Brazilians in your team in terms of building trust, because this will not be the same as it would be with your Japanese colleagues.

Adapting your leadership style to the people around you and asking how you, as the leader, can navigate a multi-cultural setting is the foundation of cultural intelligence. This goes beyond your team; in a multi-national setting it is about understanding the markets, your customers and the differences in organisational cultures, including what is perceived as good leadership in a given culture. What is defined as good leadership in one society will definitely not be considered good leadership in another society, as many people working in multi-national companies can confirm.

How a lack of cultural intelligence harms organisations

Let us flip the coin for a moment and look at what cultural un-intelligence looks like. We carried out an inclusion survey for a multi-national company, which was headquartered in Denmark.

The findings of this survey revealed that those working at locations away from the headquarters perceived a high degree of ethnocentrism at the Danish headquarters. This resulted in the employees away from the head-quarters feeling an "out-of-sight, out-of-mind" syndrome.

When we presented the findings, this was a surprise to those in top management, many of whom were Danes. They were unaware, for example, that high-ranking, non-Danish leaders felt that they had very little chance to join the executive team at the headquarters. As one of the respondents said: "You have to be five times better than a Dane to get his job."

Another significant finding from this inclusion survey was that the respondents based in other locations had a much lower score in relation to belonging than their colleagues at head office. One interviewee said: "This is a very Danish company that is trying to become more international. It is hindered by the lack of understanding and inclusion of other cultures that is inherent in all aspects of daily life. In particular, there is a significant issue with a lack of diversity in management and it's clear that they're doing nothing to fix it."

This was a wake-up call for the top management team. They had no idea that it was a blindspot for them. As a result of these findings in the inclusion survey, they introduced several programmes to deal with these aspects of the company's culture. On the other hand, this had been clear to thousands of their non-Danish employees for decades.

Gender intelligence

How do you encourage men and women to work together in an intelligent way? How do you harness the benefits of men and women working together? To do this effectively, you have to move away from thinking that we are all the same and instead respect our differences and work in smart ways to celebrate them.

When there is a 50/50 representation of men and women from bottom to top, that organisation is gender intelligent, provided there is a fair gender balance at every level.

In most companies, you will see gender balance, or almost a gender balance, at the entry level. However, as you move up the company, you see that gender balance diminishes or disappears completely. What I am referring to here is the proverbial leaky pipeline, where the company culture does not enable women to progress and therefore they leave or are stuck below the invisible glass ceiling.

Often you find that when you reach the top levels of an organisation, just 2% to 8% are women, even when there is a 50/50 gender balance at the entry level.

> *"There is a big difference in how a woman and a man lead. My experience is that it is more difficult to lead together with a man. There is an element of competition between the men – also towards women – whereas women are more likely to say 'Let's make it work together'. Men say that too, but what they really do is continue to fight, like alpha males who want to get noticed."*
>
> *– Female leader and respondent to an inclusion survey*

At the Living Institute, we are talking to some huge companies who have ambitions to correct this. ENGIE, for example, are going for a 50/50 gender balance by 2030 and LEGO® are going for 50/50 by 2032. They are talking about equal representation at all levels.

If you look at companies with very little representation of the underrepresented gender in top management in spite of having gender balance at entry levels, you know something is wrong and your inclusion survey will uncover what that is.

You can tell if a leader is gender intelligent by observing whether he or she acts on indications of inequality between genders, discrimination against one gender or harassment. An inclusive leader consistently reacts when confronted with discrimination, sexism or harassment.

As David Morrison, the former Chief of the Australian Army, said when he realised that sexual harassment against a female colleague had taken place in the army, "The standard you walk past is the standard you accept."[2]

Often when we hold workshops, we can see in people's eyes that they remember situations where they did not react as they probably should have.

---

[2]YouTube: Australian Chief to Sexist Soldiers: Respect Women Or GET OUT.

Everyone, of any gender, needs to feel that they are supported to feel safe. There needs to be accountability, so that if someone behaves inappropriately towards you, or harassment happens, you know it will be dealt with and you will be supported.

This problem is not one that is exclusive to women. A study from 2018 found that many men are sexually harassed if they work in a workplace with many women. This is not about pointing at one gender, but about understanding that this happens whenever there is an overrepresentation of a certain gender.[3]

Gender intelligence is a huge topic, and one that we will come back to in Chapter 11.

Generational intelligence

This is a leadership characteristic that involves working and leading across different generations based on the assumption that there are key differences between these generations that you need to know about and relate to in your leadership style and behaviour.

We currently see leaders facing challenges in terms of leading boomers, millennials and zoomers.[4]

As well as working with and across these generations, this leadership trait is about how to attract and retain people from different age groups.

I talked with a talented researcher, a zoomer, about a job opening in the Living Institute recently. She was doing research on the #MeToo movement,

---

[3]Rugulies, R., et al. (2018), "Onset of workplace sexual harassment and subsequent depressive symptoms and incident depressive disorder in the Danish workforce".
[4]Boomers (born between 1946 and 1964), Millennials (born between the mid 1980s and the mid 1990s), Zoomers (born between the late 1990s and early 2000s).

feminism and how our patriarchal societies were falling apart and becoming more and more divisive. I found it utterly fascinating to hear her thoughts, many of them new to me in the way she framed them. I felt I could learn a lot from her and that it would also be beneficial for our clients if we had her on board. At the end of our talk, I asked her if she would join my team. She looked at me with pity and said quietly, "No I won't. You see, we are waiting for you (boomers) to die, while we eat popcorn." I think I blinked a couple of times and I could not help smiling. It was clear to me where this came from.

In her mind, generations older than hers had corrupted societies and the planet. We are unable and unwilling to fix things, so younger generations are waiting for us to disappear so they can take over and save the planet. In actual fact, I understood every word she was saying and, looking at it from her perspective, working for me would be like working for the enemy. Would I have had the skills to lead her if she had said yes to the job? I am not sure, but I know I, as a leader, have to figure it out.

Being conscious

An inclusive leader is aware of how much unconscious bias influences all decision-making processes. They are aware that unconscious bias is the biggest barrier to diversity and inclusivity. What sets inclusive leaders apart is that they act on this knowledge.

This is perfectly summed up by a leader who completed one of our inclusion surveys, when he said, "I took a bias test and became aware. I didn't think I was biased and I was very surprised by the results of the test. Then I attended unconscious bias training and I learned that every time you have to make a decision or a choice, you are not unprejudiced. It has made me recruit more women, although it is not only about biases against men and women, it is about many things."

We will dive into unconscious bias, and how to become conscious of it and minimise it, in Chapter 9.

Humility, empathy, cultural intelligence, gender intelligence, generational intelligence and being conscious are the traits that characterise an inclusive, diversity intelligent leader.

When it comes to diversity intelligence, one of the key competencies of an inclusive leader is to use factual knowledge based on scientific research to understand what it takes to engage and motivate teams with a high degree of diversity and to apply this in their teams and organisation.

An inclusive leader creates a culture where everyone understands and accepts that they are accountable for their actions. Perhaps most importantly, they demonstrate accountability for creating a cultural transformation. Other people can look to them and clearly see that they are leading the way towards greater inclusion. This sense of personal responsibility and accountability is a key catalyst for cultural transformation.

Similarly, an inclusive leader also knows that they have to act on signs of discrimination or harassment and, just as importantly, they know how to act appropriately in such situations.

What an inclusive leader might look like

There was one story that came from a participant at one of our training sessions that really struck me. She talked about a newly appointed CEO who moved to another country, bringing his family with him, to work at the company's headquarters.

He prepared a one-hour presentation about his vision for the company, what types of commercial goals they were aiming for, what products they would need to build to improve the company in the future and so on. The night before his first day at this job, he was going through the presentation with his wife and asked what she thought. Her reply was, "Why don't you just talk about who you are?"

Immediately this idea made sense to him, so he threw away his business-focused presentation and the next day he simply talked about himself. He told his story, shared pictures of his family and even talked about how his wife had survived cancer and how that affected him and his family.

There were about 500 people present for his presentation and when he finished speaking they gave him a standing ovation.

This is a really powerful statement of what happens when a leader makes him or herself vulnerable and tells everyone at the organisation that, first and foremost, we want human beings to work here, with all their complexities. This is what we encourage. This is the kind of culture I want to create in my company. This is what motivates me. Once you have said that, you do not have to say anything else because people are automatically attracted to that kind of culture.

His decision to tell his story created a real stir in the company, and outside it. People started actively seeking to work there because they wanted to work for this person.

What this CEO communicated by telling his own story was that being human takes priority over being a business animal.

The need for inclusive leadership

One of the reasons why there can be problems in diverse teams is a lack of leadership. If no one is responsible and accountable for creating structured processes that help everyone on the team to navigate and work with these differences in a way that is beneficial, you are not likely to see the inclusive behaviours.

It can help to think of diversity as a really strong hot sauce: it can make a dish taste really good but you have to use it with caution. Diversity is the same. It has to be respected and used by someone who knows what it is and how to deal with it, otherwise it can create issues or, if we think of it like hot sauce, even ruin the flavour of the dish. This is where stereotypes, them-and-us tendencies, covering and unconscious bias can all come into play.

These issues all arise simply because there is not someone who is accountable and who has the knowledge and skill to manage diversity in an inclusive way.

Why inclusive leaders are important for businesses

From a business perspective, inclusive leaders can navigate uncertainty and adapt. These leaders know they cannot predict and control the future in this VUCA world. Instead, they sense and respond, which enables them to navigate through uncertainty and innovate when radical changes occur. Recent examples of radical changes include the Covid-19 pandemic, the financial crisis of 2008, etc.

As a result of their ability to navigate this uncertainty and adapt, companies with inclusive leaders have much greater staying power than those without.

How do leaders become inclusive leaders?

If your company wants all its leaders to become consistent, inclusive leaders, it might be a good idea to introduce an inclusive leadership programme or modules on inclusive leadership in existing programmes.

Recognising that inclusive leadership does not just happen on its own is a crucial first step. It requires deliberate work to improve people's inclusive leadership competencies. Any process to help a leader become more inclusive has to begin with a sense of understanding themselves.

Once you have developed a deep self-awareness by exploring who you are as an individual and how your history, life experiences and even the society you were raised in have affected this, you can begin working on cultivating the characteristics of an inclusive leader outlined above.

At the Living Institute, we have taken these characteristics, as well as the key traits of an inclusive leadership style, and put them into a formula. This formula is, in essence, about achieving a high level of diversity intelligence in teams led by inclusive leaders.

We have transformed our research and experiences from 17 years of working in the D&I field into a leadership programme: *Inclusive Leadership – claim the future.*

An overview of "Inclusive Leadership – claim the future"

This programme helps the participants to develop the knowledge and skills that are needed to initiate a fundamental cultural transformation in their organisation, ultimately leading to improved diversity intelligence.

There are four modules on the "Inclusive Leadership – claim the future" leadership programme. The participants in the four modules are divided into "tribes" and presented with virtual challenges, dilemmas, games and competitions, followed up with debriefing, coaching and training.

The four modules on the programme are:

- *"The New Leadership Paradigm": workshop activities based on individuals' profile analysis, covering, conscious leadership, building trust and understanding the power of opposites.*
- *"Deep Dive into the Science of Creating Innovative Cultures of Inclusion": here we dig into science, best practice and the latest research on diversity intelligence, cocooning, covering, how to reduce unconscious*

bias, advance gender balance and infuse diversity intelligence in the workplace.

- *"Building Strategies for Creating a Culture of Inclusion": two days of navigating the minefields of exclusion and homogeneity. We cover topics such as how to win the global war for talent and the knowledge of change management, as well as using LEGO® Serious Play® methodology to map present and future diversity in teams.*

- *"Hackathon: Hacking into the Future of Leadership and Innovation": a business marathon of facilitated mapping and testing your best leadership ideas. During this module, we test and adjust the individual strategies developed in module three, as well as carrying out an individual profile analysis of inclusive competencies. We also explore management 3.0 – the future of work and management.*

The programme also covers connected subjects, including how to lead teams characterised by diversity in age, cultural and educational background, ethnicity, sexual orientation, religion and cultural intelligence for organisations operating internationally.

It is also worth noting that we strongly recommend that any managers who have participated in previous leadership programmes that did not include this diversity element are offered these modules as an add-on to their training.

Highlighting the need for inclusive leadership – Part 2

Think back to the beginning of this chapter, when I asked you to imagine what an inclusion survey might show at a multi-national organisation where 80% of the leaders and managers are *not* practising inclusive leadership.

Based on studies, our own research and the inclusion surveys we have conducted in many multi-national organisations, we frequently see signs of friction and clashes when working and leading across cultures.

There are fewer women than men in the higher levels of the organisation and perhaps no women in top management.

Millennials and zoomers do not feel that they belong in that company, and therefore attracting the best talent is an issue. At the same time, boomers feel they are being left behind and not invited to the party.

There is no accountability when discrimination or incidents occur; as a result, women and minorities do not feel psychologically safe.

Diversity of thought is not welcomed, but sameness of thinking is rewarded. This comes back to the concept of cocooning, which was discussed in Chapter 4, where leaders surround themselves with a small group of people who think the same way that they do and, by unconsciously doing so, exclude others.

Do you remember the story I told you at the beginning of Chapter 3, about the woman who was referred to as "my predecessor's bitch" in one organisation that we worked with? I'd just like to share with you another quote from that same survey, from another woman who worked at that organisation and had subsequently left.

She shared the story in much the same way as the other woman, noting that both the newly appointed manager and a senior leader were showing the other man around the office when the new manager made the offensive comment. She added, "What hurt the most was that the senior leader didn't react. He too was laughing. This is why I left the company."

This comes back to the quote I shared earlier in this chapter from the Australian general David Morrison: "The standard you walk past is the standard you accept."

Predict and control vs sense and respond

As I have already said, 10 out of 10 CEOs that we speak to say that inclusion of diversity is a business-critical issue. This has only been exacerbated by Black Lives Matter and the Covid-19 pandemic. LEGO® recently told us that, because of Black Lives Matter, inclusion of diversity has become the third highest priority in the company's strategy in the coming years.

What this basically comes down to is adapting and navigating as societies and markets change, and that change is happening more and more quickly. I am sure that there will be thousands of studies about the Covid-19 pandemic and how it affected companies.

At the time of writing, we are seeing some companies growing exponentially during this pandemic and others suffering enormously.

I am certain that if you look at the traits of the companies in each of these two categories you will find that the ones that are growing have adapted, have the innovation muscles to do so and have turned this into an added advantage. Meanwhile, the companies that are struggling will be characterised by a sameness of thinking and a conviction that they will do what they have always done.

It comes down to some companies opting to predict and control; these are the companies that will struggle to survive. Others are opting to sense and respond; these are the companies that will not only survive but thrive.

Those who sense what is going on in the present, who know they need to do something and respond, will survive.

LEGO® is an excellent example. They have sensed that they need to know more about Black Lives Matter and know that they need to respond for the good of their business. This ability to sense what is going on around the world is particularly important, because LEGO® is located in a small village on the west coast of Jutland in Denmark where there are no black people. However, because their business is global, they have sensed that they need to respond.

Summary

Inclusive leadership is essential at every level to bring about a sustainable cultural transformation within your organisation and to enable your business to harness the power of the diversity within your teams. We have explored the key traits that inclusive leaders share, and looked at how you can start developing these characteristics within yourself.

Being aware and conscious of your behaviour and thought processes is an essential first step. As we know, there is a lot going on in our unconscious minds and it takes a deliberate effort to counteract that. The key thing to remember, however, is that anyone can become an inclusive leader with dedication and effort.

In the next chapter, we are going to explore the important role that D&I Champions play in bringing about that cultural transformation – but to enable them to have a meaningful impact, it will be essential to have inclusive leadership.

Chapter 8

D&I Champions: Supporting Cultural Transformation

A n important part of developing diversity and creating gender balance within organisations is having the right support functions to support the managers and leaders in the transition.

It is also essential to have people who can lead on the executive committee's vision and not only implement the D&I strategy but also know what to look for and how to react to the findings of the annual inclusion surveys. Every organisation needs to have this kind of task force and we call them D&I Champions.

The D&I Champions are the backbone of the support function. The D&I agenda has to be anchored in top management, as already discussed. Those in top management need to allocate the budget to implement the D&I strategy they set out. That might involve money for the correct training, or to change processes or procedures.

Why you need D&I Champions

The executive team on its own is not in a position to make the kinds of wholesale changes that are required to implement an effective D&I strategy. They need a task force to implement their strategy and vision. Needless to say, this task force needs to be educated to ensure each D&I Champion has the knowledge and tools to skilfully support managers and employees in creating a culture of inclusion.

Within any organisation, doubt will crop up frequently and help will be needed. Managers will be faced with targets and will need support from skilled D&I Champions in recruitment and internal career development.

These advisers must have the authority, competence, knowledge and skills to change the old culture and be valuable partners in the processes that need to change.

Educated change-makers are top management's guarantee that the new D&I strategy is on every business agenda, across every aspect of daily life within an organisation. If people are not equipped with the knowledge and tools, then personal responsibility will weaken, excuses will flourish and old habits will win again.

Why educate D&I Champions?

You cannot simply pick a few people and suddenly make them D&I Champions. They have to adopt this role after undergoing education in the field of diversity and inclusion.

As Susanne Broman, VP Global Talent Management and People Development at Alfa Laval Corporate AB said after having attended a D&I Champion Certification programme: "You can read all the books and hear the many talks about D&I, but what I took away from this intensive training was a whole picture and a frame based on research and facts. It has given me the capabilities to move the agenda forward."

Susanne signed up with one of her colleagues, but admits she did so mostly out of curiosity. However, she found there were more benefits than she initially imagined. "We have gained a lot from joining the programme together. Now we have the same competencies, knowledge and point of origin. We are aligned on the initiatives and the right steps moving forward. We are tapping into the same source of knowledge and competences," she explained.

She also revealed that she learned to communicate differently through this training. "The programme simply gave us data, a language and a platform to work from; enabling us to have the conversation on a qualified level without the blame game and escalating conflicts. I am not being caught on the wrong foot – I stand strong," Susanne said.

It has also helped her to realise that there is much more to D&I than minority groups. She noted, "The D&I Certification made it clear that we shouldn't focus on the minority groups and put people into boxes. Instead, we focus on the majority because they need to understand what's going on, and their role in it."

One initiative that really resonated with her, and that she has found to be most effective, is that of mobilising men. "Without them we won't succeed in this transformation," she asserted.

Susanne feels that completing the programme has given her the ability to fast-forward the agenda at her organisation and she is already seeing results. "Based on what we learned, we have now trained 18 facilitators ready to train our management teams."

She also has a clear understanding of the business imperative for D&I. "Without inclusion of diversity companies won't survive. It is critical for all companies to be able to attract younger generations," she said, before adding, "10 years from now it shouldn't be necessary to talk about diversity anymore. It should just be a given that we are all different and we are all important."

The primary reason to educate your D&I Champions is to develop deep diversity competencies in this selected group of HR professionals, business partners, key personnel and change-makers, so that they are prepared to have a daily dialogue with managers and fulfil the ambitious goals being set surrounding D&I. All of your D&I Champions will therefore be acting on a clearly communicated mandate from top management.

Once trained, they will know how to handle the challenges and issues that will inevitably pop up and how to tackle resistance and mobilise everyone.

Often, when we look for people to train as D&I Champions, we discover that the necessary skills and knowledge do not already exist within an organisation. Of course, in some cases they might. However, when we talk to the people within HR departments who are responsible for the D&I agenda, we are often surprised by how few tools they have to move it forward, and how little they know about the topic.

Our experiences at the Living Institute raised the question, how can we make companies even more inclusive if nobody in the organisation has the skills or knowledge they need? This is why we created a course to educate D&I Champions, teaching them how to orchestrate a cultural transformation.

It is a comprehensive programme. The attendees are given homework and we follow up on what they do. The feedback we have received from participants is extremely positive and we are already seeing them create miracles in their organisations.

"It's the most comprehensive and qualitatively most demanding course I've seen so far on the topic of D&I!

I wish I had visited your Masterclass two years ago when I started to work on this topic and designed the lectures for my Business master students.

I would definitely recommend the Masterclass to HR Managers and D&I Managers working in multicultural companies, as well as to change agents and consultants facilitating D&I in their organisations!"
– Aleksandra, D&I Expert, Germany, D&I Champion Feb. 2020

"It was a great experience for me, I really enjoyed every module, and I'm back now with a lot of practical knowledge to implement in Chile."
– Marilen Corbalan, HR Consultant, Chile,
D&I Champion Feb. 2020

"A very comprehensive course with an extraordinary amount of expert knowledge giving lots of food for thought about how to work with D&I in your own organisation. I will definitely recommend this Masterclass to others!"
– Tina Schelle, Communications, Danish Composers' Society,
D&I Champion Nov. 2020

"Very clear overall and also hands-on tools to drive the D&I agenda, especially with the wheel[1] and also the flexibility which is needed to jump between the four quarters from time to time."
– Nadine, Global Business Partner, Denmark,
D&I Champion Feb. 2020

---

[1] See Part 2 introduction.

Once they are back in their organisations, they tell us that the course has made the world of difference to them because they know the mechanisms, as well as the dos and don'ts, to launch impactful diversity intelligence initiatives. As a result, they are supporting the whole organisation in achieving outstanding results.

This is particularly important in today's internationally competitive world, where companies want to not only attract the greatest and most diverse talent, but also retain them. To keep these people at your organisation you have to create a culture of inclusion, and D&I Champions will help you to do that.

What characteristics do D&I Champions need?

It is important that your D&I Champions are passionate about the agenda. This is one of the most essential qualities for these people to have, and often you find people who are most passionate about D&I in HR.

The natural place for D&I Champions to be based is within the HR department. There are several reasons why this typically works well. Firstly, because HR would normally deal with issues relating to diversity and inclusivity. Secondly, because after the training they know how to create recruitment processes free of unconscious bias. Thirdly, as HR professionals, they already serve as a support function to units and managers. Finally, because they will be working closely with the head of HR, who will play an important role in the development and implementation of any D&I strategy.

On a more personal level, a D&I Champion needs to be someone with an understanding of the whole system of an organisation, as well as their role within it, which is why those with an HR background are a good fit.

Unless you have a very small company, you need to have multiple D&I Champions to form your task force.

D&I Champions will be implementing your D&I strategy, so they will need to educate and train others within your organisation. When you are looking for people to be D&I Champions, it can be beneficial to choose people who have training skills, because part of their role will involve delivering training to others.

Another key aspect of a D&I Champion's role is to assist with the facilitation of the annual inclusion survey. This involves sending out emails, organising interviews and focus groups – what you might call the "behind the scenes" work.

D&I Champions also need to understand the many different diversity parameters and what needs to be put in place at an organisation to enhance diversity. They need to be aware of, and understand, cultural intelligence and know the signs of cultural un-intelligence, as well as when there is a need for training. This is particularly important in multinational companies. They do not necessarily need to provide the training, but they have to feel confident they can identify any issues that arise.

They will also understand the mechanisms of gender imbalance and know the signs to look for and the myths they need to address and counter.

In addition, to enhance inclusivity, the level of trust, psychological safety and belonging among minority groups, the D&I Champions need to understand the dynamics of power and privilege and how everyone can be equally represented at all levels.

What do D&I Champions do?

At the beginning of this part of the book, I outlined the four steps that organisations need to take to create a diverse and inclusive culture. Although D&I Champions can support Steps 1 to 3, it is really Step 4: Action, where they have the greatest involvement.

However, D&I Champions know this circle of steps inside out. They know why an organisation has to start at Step 1, the drive. They understand the importance of gathering information and getting the knowledge base they need in Step 2, before developing a strategy in Step 3. D&I Champions can support each of these steps, but it is not their role to lead on those first three steps; that has to come from top management.

When we reach Step 4, however, well-trained D&I Champions are well placed to take action and implement the strategy across an organisation.

It is essential that D&I Champions understand all the steps in this process, as well as how each step has been executed at their organisation. Their knowledge will come through in their conversations with colleagues and managers and they are happy to share it.

Building trust and creating psychological safety for everyone in an organisation is one of the most important aspects of a D&I Champion's role. Psychological safety is for everyone, not only for minorities, because those who are in the majority will also have concerns and might be worried about what the D&I strategy means for their role in the company. In our workshops, white middle-aged men often tell me that they know diversity does not refer to them and that they feel like the villain. It is important that their voices are not lost among everything else that is going on. A D&I Champion is aware that equality feels like discrimination for those who are privileged.

What do D&I Champions need to know?

There are certain topics that D&I Champions have to be familiar with if they are to be effective, all of which are covered in the course that we offer. At a top level, they are:

- The business case for diversity intelligence.
- The drivers and barriers for inclusion, diversity and gender balance.
- Implementing data-based solutions.
- Familiarisation with inclusive leadership.
- To create a language around unconscious bias.
- Accelerating gender balance, including the 13 dos and four don'ts for creating gender balance.
- The mechanisms and dynamics of inclusion, which involves building trust and creating psychological safety.
- Designing a transformational D&I roadmap covering all aspects of the cultural transformation.

Hacking the company culture

To improve diversity, inclusion and gender balance within an organisation requires identification of the barriers in the existing culture. Part of a D&I Champion's role is to hack these elements in the company culture and bridge these gaps.

To do this effectively, D&I Champions need to know what elements of the existing company culture are producing these imbalances and discrimination in order to then "hack" them.

The way we approach this in our programme at the Living Institute is to use LEGO® Serious Play® as a strategic tool to get each person to build a mini D&I strategy. Although D&I Champions are not the people who have responsibility for creating the overall D&I strategy at their organisations, as this responsibility rests with the executive team and HR director, this exercise allows us to check that they have mastered the whole process.

D&I Champions and their relationship with top management

D&I Champions have to work alongside the executive team to bring about a cultural change. What has been encouraging is that the D&I Champions we have trained often come back to us to get us to run training sessions with the executive team.

It shows not only that the board is allocating a budget to advancing the D&I agenda, but also that everyone understands their roles and they are all taking responsibility for their part in executing the D&I strategy.

We have also noticed that the dynamic between the board and the D&I Champions who make up the task force is greatly improved after the D&I Champions have been trained. Before, both parties agreed that the issue was business critical, but generally neither one really knew what to do. I know this has resulted in quite a few frustrating conversations for both sides.

Once the D&I Champions were trained, these conversations became much easier and led to better strategies made in unison. Frankly, I sense a clarity and ease when this alignment is manifested. I am still amazed by the magnitude of the before-and-after effects this has.

Summary

Embedding D&I Champions throughout your organisation is essential for your D&I strategy to gain traction on the ground and for the initiatives you are introducing to be implemented effectively.

However, D&I Champions need to be properly educated and trained to allow them to fulfil their role, and those in top management need to be aware that D&I Champions are there to support their D&I strategy, not to create it and take responsibility for it.

I have mentioned unconscious bias training as part of what we focus on with D&I Champions. This is what we are going to explore in much greater detail in the next chapter.

Chapter 9

Unconscious Bias

U nconscious bias is one of the biggest barriers to diversity and inclusion. It leads to bad decision-making and missed opportunities to attract talent to an organisation. This is why it is such a hot topic and why we need to run unconscious bias training.

What is unconscious bias?

In short, unconscious bias is the brain guessing and blinding you to factual information. Since it is unconscious, you are not normally aware of it. You do not realise you have these biases and you do not see them. To most people, they are invisible until you identify them; then you begin to see them everywhere.

Through unconscious bias training, the aim is to identify these biases and to minimise them in your decision-making, recruitment and relations to other people.

Unconscious bias happens because our brains are constantly seeking out mental shortcuts to save energy and make decisions quickly. These shortcuts are based on stereotypical notions of other people, as well as preferences and prejudice. They are based on, and reflected in, the society we grew up in, the companies we have worked for and our social relationships throughout our lives.

What all of this means is that we are prone to be unconsciously biased towards what our brain already knows. In other words, unconscious bias makes us reproduce the past.

Why is unconscious bias a problem?

The problem with unconscious bias is that it leads to unintentional stereotyping and discrimination, both positive and negative, even if we believe and tell ourselves that we are rational and behave objectively and treat people equally.

Because unconscious bias makes us prone to repeating the past, it is important that we overcome it if we want to create a different future. If it is left unchecked, we lose the ability to avoid its unwanted effects of repeating the past.

To overcome this, we need to use our brains differently; think fast and slow. This concept of thinking fast and slow comes from Daniel Kahneman and is thoroughly explored in his international bestselling book *Thinking, Fast and Slow*.[1]

Who needs unconscious bias training?

Everyone can benefit from unconscious bias training. Usually the target groups for this training include all the employees and managers in an

---

[1]Kahneman, D. (2012), *Thinking, Fast and Slow*, Penguin.

organisation who are involved in recruitment processes, decision-making, working on the front line meeting customers, leading others, developing products, facilitating team member interviews, processing key HR jobs and those who have communication responsibilities.

We find that people in these roles benefit from understanding how unconscious bias influences decision-making.

What is unconscious bias training?

Unconscious bias training gives participants the tools they need to recognise and minimise their personal biases and to see how unconscious bias inappropriately affects their work and cooperation.

The training also teaches them what language to use when talking about biases and how they can address the issues they encounter as a result of either their own, or someone else's, biases.

Unconscious bias training acknowledges that everyone makes bad decisions sometimes. Well-designed, expert unconscious bias training will cover the following:

- An awareness of the fact that we all have unconscious bias and why we have it.
- Knowledge of what unconscious bias is and typical examples of where it occurs.
- Knowledge about why unconscious bias leads to poor decision-making.
- What constructive language you can use to talk about unconscious bias without blaming one another.
- Specific tools to identify unconscious bias and reduce the adverse effects it has in real life situations.

However, unconscious bias training alone will not do the trick. Despite its ability to change the mindset and create a higher degree of self-reflection, if the fundamental culture, overall structures and processes remain unchanged, then the effect will be minimal.

> *"I attended a workshop on unconscious bias and it was an eye-opener in relation to a subject which is otherwise difficult to handle. Because the workshop was professionally executed, the participants left the workshop with a better understanding of themselves and their workplace."*
>
> *– Female leader of leaders, Ministry of Foreign Affairs*

Potential issues resulting from poorly delivered unconscious bias training

Unfortunately, this training can have negative consequences if it is not delivered with great caution and competence. At worst, poor unconscious bias training may have the opposite effect and could potentially strengthen existing stereotypes.

When this kind of training is poorly delivered, it can make people feel as though there is nothing they can do about their unconscious bias. In some cases it can act as an excuse to keep doing what they have always done and provide people with a reason not to change or improve their decision-making processes.

There is a great deal of discussion about whether unconscious bias training is effective or not. However, if you look at the instances where it has worked and has had a positive effect, it is because the training is well designed and delivered with a great deal of expertise.

Resistance to unconscious bias training

It is not uncommon for people to resist the concept of unconscious bias or to push back and believe that it is a problem that others have, rather than them.

There are more than 150 unconscious biases, but the most important one to identify is the one we call the *über bias:* "Others have it, not me. I'm rational, objective and treat everybody the same."

Interestingly, research has found that the better educated the person, the more they are in denial. I have certainly heard many people tell me that they do not have unconscious bias. They believe that they are smart enough to avoid it, that they base all their decisions on facts, but, of course, all of us have unconscious biases.

Generally, one of the challenges for people with high levels of intelligence is to admit that their brain is doing something that they do not want it to. Very often, people in this situation are used to trusting themselves and they do not believe that they make mistakes, which can make the idea of them personally holding unconscious biases hard to accept. We conduct unconscious bias workshops at universities for academic staff, as well as professors and postdocs, and we can confirm that, yes, they have these unconscious biases too.

A study that I find very interesting shows us that there is little correlation between a group's collective intelligence and the IQs of its individual members. On the other hand; if a group includes more women, its collective intelligence rises.[2]

---

[2]Malone, T.W., and Woolley, A. (2011), "The Female Factor", *Harvard Business Review*.

It is also interesting to note that women are generally more accepting of the fact that they have unconscious biases than men are. This is merely an observation I have made having facilitated unconscious bias training for thousands of people around the world.

Failing to accept your own unconscious biases can have a significant impact on your professional performance, as well as on the performance of the business you work for. If you do not accept that your decisions are influenced by what you have seen and heard before, then you are unlikely to question whether a decision is right, or whether you have another viable option. All that will happen is that you reproduce the past.

Can you spot the unconscious bias?

Read the Facebook status update below and see if you can spot any biases:

 ꝺ̵ꝷ꜠ Hashima Ai ꜠ ꝰꝼ I keep telling my grand daughters to Date the nerd in school, he may turn out to be a Mark Zuckerberg! Thanks for FB, I've reconnected with family and many old friends and classmates.
Like · Reply · 👍 4,970 · Yesterday at 5:14am

Figure 9.1 Facebook post

What did you notice? Can you see any biases? If so, what are they? Make a note below.

There are several biases in this status:

1. Assuming that a successful tech entrepreneur would be a nerd in high school.
2. Assuming that people who are considered nerds are intelligent and will end up being successful.
3. Assuming that her granddaughters cannot become successful tech entrepreneurs themselves.
4. Assuming a nerd is a man or a boy.
5. Assuming that her granddaughters would want to date a man.

What is particularly brilliant in this example is that Mark Zuckerberg actually replied directly to her post, calling out one of her biases:

 Raju w Harkarra Aras the I keep telling my grand daughters to Date the nerd in school, he may turn out to be a Mark Zuckerberg! Thanks for FB, I've reconnected with family and many old friends and classmates.
Like · Reply · 👍 4,970 · Yesterday at 5:14am

 Mark Zuckerberg ✓ Even better would be to encourage them to "be" the nerd in their school so they can be the next successful inventor!
Like · Reply · 👍 27,252 · Yesterday at 5:32am

↪ View more replies

Figure 9.2 Facebook post reply

That example is exactly what unconscious bias training is all about. It is about finding these biases all the time; hearing them and seeing them both in ourselves and in others. However, when it comes to correcting them in others, we need to use the right kind of language so that we are doing this without blame.

If unconscious bias causes problems, why do we have it?

Our brain receives 11 million bits of information per second and we can consciously process just 40 of them. That means our subconscious mind picks up the almost 11 million bits of information that our conscious mind cannot.[3]

---

[3]Mlodinov, L. (2012), *Subliminal: How Your Unconscious Mind Rules Your Behavior*, Pantheon.

To allow you to deal with all of this information, your brain creates a pattern. It can help to imagine this like a path in a forest. Think of it as though you are walking from one village to another village. To get there you have to go through a forest and you are the first person to make this journey. On that first journey, you will be very aware of every step you take and be on the lookout for any dangers and so on.

You make it safely to the other village and, as the evening is drawing in, you have to make your way back to your village. Of course, you will want to return along the route you took earlier in the day because your brain knows this is safe, so you will try to follow that same path again.

The more times you make the journey, the more a clear path will emerge through that forest. Soon, other people also start using your path to travel between the villages. Eventually there may even be a highway that cuts through the forest, so people do not even have to think about how to get from one place to the other any more. You do not have to watch where you are putting your feet or worry about obstacles. You can just walk easily and quickly.

This is a simplified explanation of what our brains do to save energy. If we had to relate to the 11 million bits of information we receive every second, we would be exhausted simply by existing. The brain needs to save energy to allow us to function and it does this by repeating what we have learned again and again.

For example, your brain knows a cup of tea could be hot when you drink it, so you are careful. However, when you have a glass of cold water, you drink it differently. You do not think about this, your brain just knows what to do based on what it has experienced in the past. You have created that clear, smooth path in your brain.

Creating pathways in the brain

Look at the image below, what do you see?

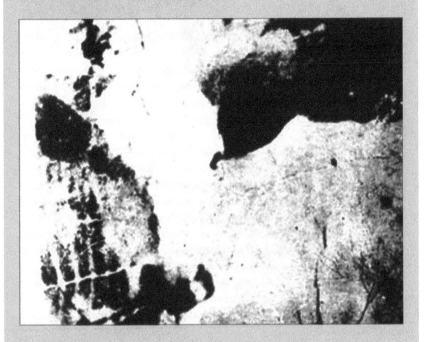

Figure 9.3 Image

What do you think it is a picture of? Take a moment to look at that image and make a note of your ideas.

What if I told you it was a photo of a cow? Can you see it now? If you look at this image again tomorrow, you will see a cow. If you look at this page in the book one year from now, you will also see a cow.

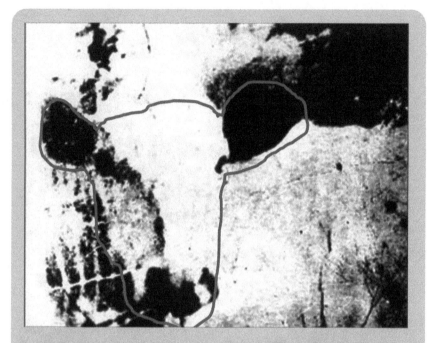

Figure 9.4 Renshaw's cow

This is how quickly we train our brain to recognise something.

Let us apply this same process to a real-world example. My grandson is two and a half years old. If I say to him, "Today we have a CEO coming", he might wonder if that is a type of food that he can eat. He might think it is a person he can play in the snow with. Or he might think it is an animal that he will be scared of.

If, when the CEO comes, he is a man in a suit, then his brain will file that information away. If the next CEO he meets is also a man in a suit, and so is the one after that, he will one day think, "Okay, if I'm ever going to hire a CEO I will go for this model."

Figure 9.5   Danish Financial Council 2014 (Photo: Peter Hove, Ritzau Scanpix)

Reference: Peter Hove Olesen/Politiken/Ritzau Scanpix

It is really difficult to see the man who is not wearing a suit in that photo, which demonstrates how hard it can be for our brain to see past its conditioning.

Stereotypes are a product of unconscious bias

This is an example of an experience I had when I was looking for a toilet in a restaurant at a hotel in Berlin. I was looking for the bathroom when I came across the door shown below.

My initial thought was that this was a unisex toilet, but the small square to the right of the door made me think again, so I carried on looking to see if I could find another door with a different symbol on it.

Figure 9.6 The men's room in Berlin Hotel

This is what I came across next:

Figure 9.7 The ladies' room in Berlin Hotel

I am a woman and I love football and I hate shopping, but still when I saw that image I thought to myself, "Okay, I'm a woman, I like shopping." We tell ourselves all the time that women like shopping and men like football, to the point that we even put it on our toilet doors, and probably insult a lot of people in the process.

Stereotyping leads to us reproducing the past. For example, research in Denmark shows that, on average, women with a non-white and non-Danish ethnic background have to send 18% more job applications to get an interview than women with a white Danish ethnic background. However, if a woman wears a headscarf indicating her Muslim identity, she has to send 60% more applications compared to the white Danish woman.[4]

Another eye-opening study relating to gender bias was carried out by Corinne Moss-Racusin, a psychologist at Yale, and her colleagues in 2012. In their randomised double-blind study, science faculties from research-intensive universities rated the application of a student – who was randomly assigned either a male name, John, or female name, Jennifer – for a laboratory manager position. Faculty participants rated John as significantly more competent and hireable than Jennifer. The participants also selected a higher starting salary for John. He would receive just over $30,000 as an annual salary, whereas Jennifer would receive $26,500 annually.

The gender of the faculty participants did not affect responses, such that female and male faculty were equally likely to exhibit bias against the female student.

The study is usually referred to as the "John and Jennifer" study.[5]

---

[4]Dahl, M. (2019), "Detecting Discrimination: How Group-Based Biases Shape Economic and Political Interactions: Five Empirical Contributions", available at: https://menneskeret.dk/sites/menneskeret.dk/files/media/dokumenter/malte_dahl_forskning.pdf.

[5]Moss-Racusin, C., et al. (2012), "Science Faculty's Subtle Gender Biases Favor Male Students", PNAS, Volume 109 (no. 41), 16474–16479, available at: https://www.pnas.org/content/pnas/109/41/16474.full.pdf.

Do you remember the data I shared with you earlier, about the survey we carried out in the financial sector? Here we found 60% of female respondents at the highest levels of management believed there was enough female talent within their organisation to address gender balance issues, compared to just 20% of male respondents from the highest levels of management.

Covering is another product of unconscious bias

We generally all know that other people may have biases against us and, as a result, we may try to cover certain sides of ourselves to fit in. We call this covering.

When we carry out our inclusion surveys, one of the things we measure is the level of covering within an organisation. Remember how I said we can all feel whether a company is inclusive or diverse when we walk in? One of the ways in which we measure this internally is by what clothes people are wearing. If everybody dresses the same way, men and women, that suggests a lack of inclusivity and diversity.

Look at the figure 9.5 again, can you see the women who are there?

There are actually a few women in that photo, but they are so hard to spot because they are wearing suits, just like the men, and they have short hair, just like the men. There are no flowery dresses or bright items of clothing. This is a classic example of covering.

In fact, the men in this photo are covering too. Why are there no men in that picture wearing a Hawaiian shirt? Because they probably believe they would lose credibility by turning up wearing a Hawaiian shirt. This is an extreme example of covering, but most of us do it.

> *"I have been working here for five years now and there are more than 4,000 people working here – and am I the only gay person? Of course I am not, but the fact that the up to 800 other gay people in this organisation are covering their sexual orientation tells me that the culture in this company is not inclusive on the contrary."*
> — *Male respondent to an inclusion survey*

When you look at who covers the most, research from Deloitte[6] found that there are certain groups of people who are covering significant sides of themselves when they go to work: 83% of LGBT individuals say they cover to a large extent, while 79% of black people, 67% of women of colour, 66% of women in general and 63% of Hispanics all say that they cover at work. Even 45% of straight white men say that they cover.

That means in the photo I just shared with you, 45% of the men in that picture probably wanted to wear something other than a suit when they got up that morning.

The problem is that the more people cover within your organisation, the less room there is to be different, and the less likely you are to attract and retain talent.

What can you do about unconscious bias?

The concepts put forward in Daniel Kahneman's book *Thinking, Fast and Slow*[7] can help us find ways to counter our unconscious bias. In his book,

---

[6]Deloitte (2019), *Uncovering Talent: A New Model of Inclusion*, available at: https://www2.deloitte.com/content/dam/Deloitte/us/Documents/about-deloitte/us-about-deloitte-uncovering-talent-a-new-model-of-inclusion.pdf.
[7]Kahneman, D. (2012), *Thinking, Fast and Slow*, Penguin.

he talks about the two different ways in which our brains make decisions: fast and slow.

Thinking fast is exactly that, we make instantaneous decisions based on the information our brain receives. Thinking slow is conscious thinking. It involves effort and thinking through something step by step in a complex process. It is the difference between looking at a photo of a baby and being able to tell if it is happy or sad, and being asked to multiply 17 by 24. You can look at a baby's face and make an instant decision about how it feels, but to reach an answer for 17 × 24 takes time and conscious thought.

When you have three candidates for CEO and you have to hire one of them, if you are thinking fast when you make that decision you will choose the man in the suit, as I mentioned earlier. However, if you do not want to have another man on your executive committee, you have to think slow. This involves asking yourself questions like, "Should I pick him, and if so, why do I pick him? What is it that I see? What is it that I don't see?"

Of course, this takes time, but that is the point. It takes time to think slow and sometimes we have to force our brains to do it to reach the right decision.

I would also recommend taking the Implicit Association tests available through Project Implicit, which is run by Harvard University. You can find these online and they allow you to uncover your beliefs and attitudes towards a range of topics, including race, skin tone, gender, disability, religion, transgender, sexuality, weight, age and many more.

This is an excellent tool for a self-assessment of your unconscious biases and one that I believe all of us can benefit from.

How can you tell if unconscious bias training is effective?

Making people aware of their unconscious biases and tackling these in the workplace takes time. We have to accept that we will always have unconscious biases, while at the same time aiming to become aware of them.

One of the ways in which you can tell that unconscious bias training has been effective is when you hear conversations about unconscious bias happening around the workplace. You want to hear people talking to their colleagues at the watercooler or over lunch about when they have identified their own biases or recognised how unconscious bias might have affected the outcome of a meeting.

When unconscious bias training is effective, you will hear conversations about unconscious bias at play constantly. This shows that people are looking to minimise their unconscious biases and that they feel comfortable talking about them. This is essential, because it allows them to have constructive conversations when they notice unconscious bias in their colleagues as well as in themselves.

If, on the other hand, you have introduced unconscious bias training and you do not hear a word about it from anybody, there is a good chance that it has not worked.

Summary

Unconscious bias is a significant topic and one that is very important to explore within your organisation as you work towards diversity intelligence at all levels. Accepting that we all have unconscious biases is the first step. Identifying what those are on an individual level, as well as at a team and an organisational level, is essential.

As I have explained, unconscious bias training can be highly effective when it is delivered correctly and will give the people within your organisation more tools to help them think slow.

In the next chapter, I will explore cultural intelligence, which is an essential element of creating a more diverse and inclusive workplace, particularly in today's multi-national world. Developing an understanding of how other cultures might be different from your own is crucial to be able to navigate in different cultural dimensions without causing offence. To enhance collaboration across borders and across nationalities, you need to operate in a culturally intelligent way.

I will explore some of the most common pitfalls and problems that people encounter when working across cultures to help you develop your cultural intelligence. Being aware of these potential issues is the key to successful collaboration.

Chapter 10

Cultural Intelligence

There are many different definitions of what cultural intelligence is, but one of my favourite definitions of cultural intelligence comes from Martha L. Maznevski, from the International Institute for Management Development. She says: "You know you are culturally intelligent when you get the reactions you expected – again and again over time."

I love her definition because it explains how you can tell when you are doing something wrong. What she is saying is that if you are in a culturally diverse setting and you never get the reactions you expect, then it is a sign that there is something you need to know and you have not adapted your behaviour to this setting.

In John's story (see below), he clearly did not get the reaction he expected from Rahul when he told him that if he did not improve his behaviour, he would be fired. In fact, you will see that John gets a real surprise when the middle manager tells him what he did to get Rahul to change his behaviour. Surprise, surprise.

A trip to Chennai

I would like to introduce you to John. He is American and works at one of America's largest banks in a senior management role. He has just been sent to Chennai, in India, for six months to work out why the company is not getting the return on investment it wanted from outsourcing IT support to the team there.

Let me share a little background to this story, before we continue to follow John. Two years ago, the bank John works for decided to outsource its IT services to an Indian company based in Chennai because management calculated that they could save a substantial amount of money by paying hourly rates to Indian IT experts rather than American IT experts.

However, they did not see the expected savings and, in fact, they were not getting the quality of work they wanted either. This is where we rejoin John, who has been sent to Chennai to find out why the IT support service was not working as expected.

In his first couple of weeks in Chennai, John spends most of his time simply observing the employees. During this period, he notices one young and very talented IT expert named Rahul, who has great potential but who barely seems to do any work. He arrives late to work every day. Every time John looks up from his desk, Rahul seems to be chatting to his colleagues by the watercooler. One day John even found Rahul asleep under his desk.

He is at the end of his tether, so he calls Rahul into his office and tells him that if he does not improve his behaviour and shape up, he will have to fire him. John cannot really see what else he can do, since this is exactly what he would do if one of his team members behaved this way in America. Rahul promises that he will improve his behaviour and will start working really hard.

John keeps an eye on Rahul for the next couple of days and cannot see any change in his behaviour. He is still arriving late and spending most of his day chatting at the watercooler. John is resigned to having to fire Rahul, but just as he is about to call him into his office, one of the middle managers knocks on his office door to talk about a different matter.

While he is there, John tells him about Rahul and explains that he will have to let him go. "He's just not pulling his weight and it sets a bad example. I'm going to fire him this afternoon," John says. The middle manager smiles and says, "I understand. Could you just give me one day to see if I can fix things?" John agrees, as giving Rahul one extra day would not hurt, although he cannot imagine what the middle manager can say or do that will change Rahul's behaviour.

The next morning, Rahul arrives at work on time. He spends his whole day working like crazy at his computer, taking no breaks. John is amazed, he cannot believe the change in Rahul, so he calls the middle manager into his office and asks him, "What did you do?"

If you read the rest of this chapter carefully, maybe you will be able to figure out what the middle manager did that John did not. I promise to tell you at the end of the chapter though.

We cannot talk about cultural intelligence without also having a definition for culture itself. The late renowned Dutch sociologist Geert Hofstede defined culture as "the software of the mind". It is a great way to think about culture, because if we were to look at my iPad and your iPad we would probably find that we do not have exactly the same software or programs installed, even though the hardware is the same.

If we put those definitions together, cultural intelligence can be described as the ability to function effectively in culturally diverse settings without being surprised all the time, and that the people who grew up in the same cultural environment know the codes and norms, and therefore they also know when someone breaks them. Going back to John, he is not functioning effectively as a manager in India. In fact, he is failing as a manager in this new environment. There is something they know that he does not.

The business case for cultural intelligence

In today's international world, cultural intelligence is a necessity. In many companies there are cultural differences among employees, leaders and managers. The war for talent is a global war; we want the best people to work in our companies and that means they may not be of the same nationality as those at the headquarters. They could be spread around the globe and comprise multiple nationalities and cultures.

In the 17 years the Living Institute has been operating, we have observed that the companies that are culturally diverse and culturally intelligent are more successful than the companies that have cultural diversity but lack cultural intelligence. The companies that lack cultural intelligence generally find it much harder to harness the benefits that cultural diversity brings.

We can back this observation up with the data that we have collected from our inclusion surveys. For example, in a survey conducted at a French company, we might hear statements from their non-French employees who say that even though they work harder and are even smarter, they do not get promoted to the same extent as their French colleagues. In this case, we can surmise that non-French employees are not considered to be as talented as their French counterparts. All the non-French employees and managers are aware of this, but their French colleagues probably are not. That is the thing about privilege, those who have it are blind to it.

Statements like this show us that there is an issue at this company when it comes to navigating a culturally diverse setting in a culturally intelligent way. The company's management is blind to talent, and this might not be confined to an issue relating to nationality; it could also be the case with gender or other aspects of diversity.

The data from our surveys also often highlights ethnocentrism at an organisation's headquarters. For example, we work with a French company that has its headquarters in Paris but operates internationally. Training their leaders, French and non-French, we see and hear from people based in locations outside France who say, "They don't see us, they don't hear us, they don't seem to care much about us, and I definitely won't ever get a job on the executive committee in Paris because I'm not French."

What is also interesting at this company is that we were generally seeing low levels of inclusion among expats. However, the one exception was among expats who have come from the headquarters, such as a French worker who is now based in Brazil. These people typically feel included and do not have an issue with being an expat and working for this company outside of France because they are French. That alone gives them a higher rank.

This indicates that, if you are ambitious, it is good to be French. As a result of this perception among their non-French employees, this organisation probably loses talented and ambitious leaders and managers because they are aware, they probably do not have a future in this organisation.

All of this data shows that when large, multinational corporations work to improve diversity, they need to adjust their initiatives to local norms and cultures to have success. It pays to understand that what works in Rio does not work in Stockholm.

Striking the right balance

One of the biggest challenges for multinational organisations is a lack of awareness that they even have these issues surrounding cultural diversity. In many cases, a company's culture is inextricably linked to a place and, as a result, it often requires external assistance to see the problems and start to deal with them in a constructive way.

The key is to strike the right balance when you are navigating cultural intelligence. You do not want to lose the core values and purpose of the company by throwing the baby out with the bathwater. In most cases, this is not about making wholesale changes, but rather about adapting your ways of doing things to fit local norms and rules.

When in Rome. . .

We all know the saying, "When in Rome, do as the Romans do" and it is particularly applicable to cultural intelligence. The rules follow the location, and being culturally intelligent means that you have an eye for the fact that cultural norms and rules are linked to the territory you are working in.

Let us take John's case as an example. He cannot change the rules of what good leadership is to 1.3 billion Indians, so he will have to become acquainted with the norms in that location and then he can try to adapt and adjust. However, John cannot pretend to be Indian. There is a balance that he has to strike between being aware of what is perceived to be weak management in India and adapting accordingly without becoming Indian (which is something he can never achieve).

In this situation, the key is humility. John has to be able to say, "Okay, maybe I don't have all the right answers to everything in this world just because I'm American." He has to be humble enough to understand that he has to change or adapt his behaviour, rather than expecting those around him to adapt their behaviour and respond to his American form of management.

Cultural intelligence is a skill

Cultural intelligence (or CQ) can be measured, just like we can measure our IQ and emotional intelligence (EQ). There are various ways to measure CQ. Here at the Living Institute, we prefer to measure CQ with the Dutch profile analysis Intercultural Readiness Check. Without going into too much detail, when we are measuring CQ we are basically looking for mental flexibility.

People who are culturally intelligent are typically not stuck in a pattern of believing that their way is the only right way to be. They also have the courage to try something different, even if it is not something they are used to.

Those who are culturally intelligent think it is fun, educational and beneficial to work and interact with people from different cultures.

Flexibility is a keyword in terms of cultural intelligence. This is not like learning to do maths, where you can check an answer book and see that two plus two will always equal four. Not all Italians/Americans/Germans/Japanese people are the same. They have fellow countrymen and countrywomen who like to break the norms.

For example, if you meet one Italian and stereotype them, saying, "All Italians are like this so this is how I'm going to navigate management in Italy," you will fail, because, of course, not all Italians are the same.

When we measure cultural intelligence, we also look for people who are humble and courageous enough to constantly check whether they are on the right path.

We all know people who are culturally intelligent by nature. They are intuitively culturally intelligent. If you work in a multi-national environment and look around your organisation, you can probably already think of two or three people who you would describe as being culturally intelligent. These are the people who seem to just know how to behave with people from any culture. If you have travelled with them, you might have seen them seamlessly transition into a new cultural environment.

These people you are thinking of now are able to navigate in any cultural context with an easiness that makes everyone in the room feel comfortable. It is as if they are blind to the fact that they are communicating and interacting with people who are hardwired with different cultural norms than they themselves are.

Most of us have also met people who are the opposite of culturally intelligent. They have the opposite effect on the atmosphere in a room. Many of us have also been the one who put their foot in their mouth when interacting with people from different cultural backgrounds.

Sometimes we are able to see when someone else is constantly making mistakes in a cultural setting different from their own. Many of us will also be able to look back on moments where we have now realised that our behaviour was culturally unintelligent, even if we were unaware of it at the time.

Not for sale

This is a story about two Danish colleagues, a man and a woman, who were on a business trip in the Middle East for a global pharmaceutical company. One thing you need to know before I go any further is that we Danes use irony a lot, and it can get us into all kinds of trouble, as you will soon see.

The Danish colleagues were meeting with an Arab client and, at the end of the meeting, the client approached the man and said, "I really like your colleague, she's lovely." The Danish man jokingly replied, "You can have her. $10,000 and she's yours." They left the meeting and he didn't think anything else of it.

The next morning, five black cars arrived at the hotel where the Danes were staying and a group of men came into the hotel and approached the two Danes while they were having breakfast. The woman, completely oblivious, asked her colleague if he knew what they wanted. Then the penny dropped and he realised they were there to collect his colleague! One of the men even asked where they should transfer the $10,000.

They somehow got out of the predicament (needless to say, he did not sell his colleague), but they certainly had to forget about doing business with that client.

Cultural parameters to be aware of

There are a number of cultural parameters that can be at play in any given situation, and I am going to explore the ones that typically prove challenging when working across cultures.

Power distance: high or low?

A low-power-distance culture is one where there is a relatively high level of equality among citizens. The following story demonstrates the difference between a high-power-distance culture and a low-power-distance culture, as well as why it is important to be aware of how other people work in this regard.

Can I go to the bathroom please?

A leader in a low-power-distance culture was having a virtual meeting with an IT employee from a high-power-distance culture. At one point during the meeting, the IT expert asked the manager if he could have a bio break. Jokingly, the manager replied, "No, you'll have to wait." The meeting ran over a little, then it ended. A couple of hours later, the manager received an email from the IT expert saying, "Can I please go to the bathroom now?"

This is an extreme example of how having high- and low-power distance at a company can cause issues. As with the earlier example of the sales representatives, this story also shows why we have to be careful when using irony or sarcasm in our interactions with people from different cultures.

Time perception: monochronic or polychronic

In monochrome societies, being on time is considered incredibly important, although a great deal of the world is what we call polychronic, where this is considered less important. For example, if you get a bus in Mexico you are unlikely to find a timetable at the bus stop, because the bus simply leaves when it is full. However, in Berlin you would expect the bus to leave on time and, in fact, you would probably be frustrated if it did not.

Japan is typically a very monochronic society with its time perception, to the point where one Japanese rail company once issued a public apology because one of its trains left one minute earlier than scheduled.

Being aware of how people in other cultures perceive time and punctuality is helpful when working internationally. For example, you can see how easy it could be to cause offence by arriving late for a meeting with a team in Japan – almost as much as arriving too early.

Communication style: direct or indirect?

Do you say things as they are, or do you try to beat around the bush? In a culture that typically has a direct communication style, it is impolite to be indirect, and vice versa. In a direct culture like the Netherlands or Denmark, we want people to get to the point. However, in an indirect culture it is considered very rude to behave like this. Small talk, pre-meetings and other social activities, such as karaoke, may all form part of the communication and relationship-building process in an indirect culture.

Collectivism vs individualism

The difference between collectivism and individualism is that in a collectivist society, you do not make important decisions alone, you confer with your family, your father, your uncles and so on for their input. The decision you make would be made collectively. Cultures such as India and the Philippines are generally collectivist. However, cultures that you could describe as Anglo-Saxon, such as America, the UK, Denmark, Germany, Australia and so on, tend to be highly individualistic.

One example to illustrate this, which I often use in workshops, is looking at marriage and long-term partners. When I run a workshop in Europe and ask the question, "Could everybody whose parents chose their partner please raise their hand?" generally nobody raises their hands.

However, when I ask the same question in India, 80–90% of those present would raise their hands and tell me that their parents chose their wonderful wife or husband.

It is conducive when working across cultures to understand both approaches. In Europe, we tend to choose a partner because we fall in love with them. However, in places like India they struggle to understand why we would make such an important decision when our judgement is clouded by having fallen in love. They cannot understand why we would not wait and marry the perfect match our parents have picked for us.

Let us bring this back to a business environment. In a collectivistic society, the company and leadership culture are typically very much like a family. Organisations in this culture will usually have a picture of their founder in reception, and the CEO is often considered a father figure by those who work for them.

An individualistic company culture works differently, and therefore what works in one environment is unlikely to work in the other.

Losing face

In some cultures, losing face is a serious concern, whereas in other cultures this is given very little importance. Think back to the example of the salesman who made a joke about selling his female colleague. I am sure that for him, the whole episode was a big joke until it was not any more. However, he lost face with the Arab client, where he would likely have been seen as a man without honour.

While losing face may not have been important to the Danish sales-man, it means he is unlikely to be able to do business with that client ever again.

How to navigate cultural intelligence: the CQ Wheel

There are four elements that you need to master to successfully navigate cultural intelligence: drive, knowledge, strategy and action. Do they sound familiar? Of course, they are the same basic steps as the wheel I shared at the beginning of Part 2, which applies to all D&I agendas.

Let us explore these four steps specifically in relation to cultural intelligence.

Drive – This is where we answer the question of why we want to master cultural intelligence. That could be for business reasons, or it could be because we want to hire the best talent available and they are not neces-sarily from the same cultural background as us. It could be both. We have to establish *why* working cross-culturally is a great idea because this gives us the motivation to change our behaviour when necessary. Someone who is culturally intelligent sees working cross-culturally as a positive thing, which enables them to learn and develop personally, as well as in a busi-ness capacity.

Knowledge – This is about how we make this work. We need to know about the cultural parameters I have just explained, such as high and low power distance, time perception, communication styles and so on. Without this knowledge, it is not possible to manage those relationships effectively. This is about more than developing our knowledge of the dos and don'ts in different cultures. It is also essential to understand the deeper values and ideas that distinguish societies, including our own. Someone who is culturally intelligent can distinguish between behaviour that is affected by personality and behaviour that is affected by culture. This is an important distinction to make, because where the behaviour of others is affected by their culture, you are unlikely to find a solution if you do not adapt your own behaviour.

Strategy – Once we have this knowledge, we can plan and adjust our behaviour accordingly. For example, you might realise that you need to have more or longer meetings with your colleagues in the Philippines than those in London, because the teams in the Philippines have an indirect communication style and you need to allow additional time for relationship building.

Someone who is culturally intelligent will check their assumptions and make sure they are not too stereotypical. He or she knows that the Filippino client might not communicate indirectly or might not need to build a relationship before he or she can do business with you. In general, however, someone from the Philippines would probably prefer an indirect approach.

Action – This is about more than simply following your strategy. It is important to acknowledge that you might not feel comfortable doing something that is new to you, so you have to be able to act in a way that does not come naturally to you without challenging your core personality to the point where you do not recognise yourself.

Someone who is culturally intelligent is able to strike this balance to allow them to embrace and work within other cultures, while remaining true to their own core identity and personality.

The CQ Wheel can be summarised as the following four stages: find the motivation, prepare for your encounter, reflect on everything you experience, and act smart in the right context.

Return to Chennai

Do you remember the story of John and the IT worker Rahul? Have you figured out what the middle manager did that John did not?

I will tell you. The middle manager simply called Rahul's mother, and she had a serious conversation with her son about changing his behaviour.

India is a collectivist society and children defer to the wisdom of their parents. In Rahul's case, the manager chose to speak to his mother because he knew that she would make sure Rahul got up on time, and that she would impress on him the importance of working hard at the office.

If Rahul lost his job, the family would likely lose face within their society, because their son was fired.

Can you also understand why John, coming from America, would not have thought to take this course of action? He did not have the knowledge of Indian culture, and even if he did, he would never have been successful in using the management tool his Indian middle manager did. Sometimes you need to be humble and ask for help from a local informant and let him/her take action.

Summary

When it comes to cultural intelligence, there is a lot to be aware of and, for most of us, being culturally intelligent does not come entirely naturally. The good news is that we can work to develop our CQ intelligence, allowing us to reap the benefits of cross-cultural working. Remember how you used to navigate seamlessly between your granny's afternoon tea and playing with your friends in the schoolyard? There were two, or more, versions of being you.

This chapter offers an introduction to cultural intelligence, but as I am sure you can appreciate, there is far more to cultural intelligence than I am able to cover in one chapter in this book.

As we move into the final chapter of Part 2, we are going to explore how to create gender balance and, perhaps most importantly, mobilise men in the process.

Chapter 11

Creating Gender Balance and Mobilising Men

Warren Buffett once said, "One of the reasons for my success was that I was only competing with half of the population. Life is a lottery. I had a 50% chance of being born female with the same IQ and talent, which would have made my career options very limited."[1]

This highlights the scale of the problem we face when it comes to gender balance. It is certainly a problem worth solving though, because once you succeed in creating gender intelligence and gender balance in your organisation, you are likely to find that many of the other problems will fade away.

---

[1]Trevett, I. (2018), "Rich and Popular. . . How Does Warren Buffet Do It?' *Platinum Business Magazine*, Issue 49:19, available at: https://education.issuu.com/platinumbusiness/docs/platinum_business_magazine_-_issue__e6cbf0b640d037/20.

However, as I touched upon earlier, with any initiatives aimed at improving gender balance or diversity, it is essential to first create an inclusive culture within your organisation. Without this cultural transformation, you will not succeed in creating gender balance at your organisation.

There is a significant financial benefit to businesses creating gender balance, as we saw in Chapter 2, *Where the Money Lies*. In addition, focusing on creating gender balance has the knock-on effect of improving diversity, with underrepresented groups typically seeing more opportunities for themselves in organisations that have gender balance.

What we are going to explore in this chapter is how you can go about creating the necessary cultural transformation in your organisation to allow women, minorities and men to thrive. There are certain initiatives that are effective at improving gender balance and, better yet, some of them are very cost-effective to implement.

Similarly, there are some initiatives that are counterproductive when it comes to creating gender balance. Sadly, these are often the initiatives businesses mistakenly turn to and, in doing so, make the situation even worse.

At the Living Institute, we have identified 13 key initiatives that have a significant positive impact on gender balance in an organisation. It is worth noting that while each initiative is effective on its own, when they are combined and introduced in the right order, their positive impact is significantly amplified. It will speed up the process significantly, enabling you to reach your goals more quickly. Earlier I used the metaphor of a sprint instead of a marathon, where you might even get lost on the way.

I will also highlight the four initiatives that we commonly see being implemented but that actually have no, or even a negative, impact on improving gender balance.

The 13 initiatives that have a positive impact on gender balance are:

1. Baseline survey and annual data monitoring.
2. Synchronisation within top management.
3. Top management taking responsibility for the equality strategy.
4. Educating D&I Champions.
5. Mobilising men.
6. Unconscious bias training.
7. Mandatory inclusive leadership training.
8. Adjusting recruitment processes.
9. Placing a focus on promotion procedures and career planning.
10. Sponsorship.
11. Quotas.
12. Clear communication.
13. Workplace flexibility.

The four initiatives that have no or a negative impact on progressing with gender balance strategies are:

1. Female networks.
2. Placing responsibility for the equality strategy with HR.
3. Mentoring.
4. Women-only leadership programmes.

Evaluating initiatives for improving gender balance

Below is a chart that shows which initiatives have the greatest impact compared to how easy or difficult they are to implement. Initiatives that are both easy to implement and that have a high impact are where you want to start. The numbers in the dots show the order in which they should be implemented.

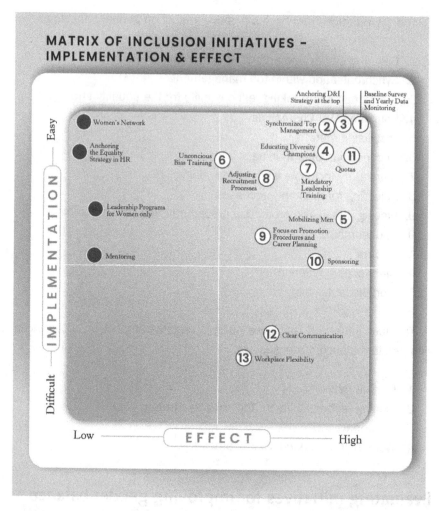

Figure 11.1 Matrix of inclusion initiatives: implementation and effect

As you can see from that chart, the four initiatives that have no or a negative effect on creating gender balance are typically easy to implement. However, when you look at the right-hand side of that chart, you can clearly see there are some very impactful initiatives that are just as easy, if not easier, to introduce than many of the ones that will set your organisation back.

In the following chart, we have also plotted the relative cost to the different initiatives against how often they are implemented in businesses. As you can see, many of the most impactful initiatives also have a low cost associated with their implementation. However, many of these are also rarely implemented.

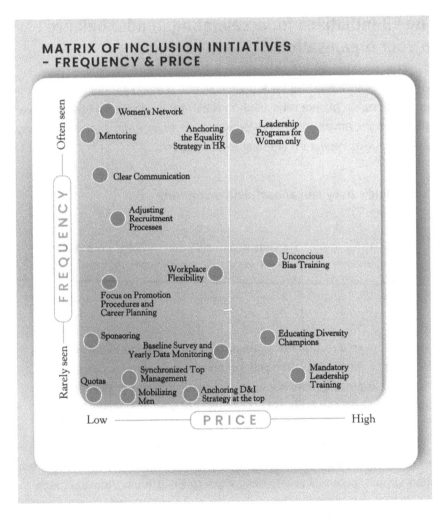

MATRIX OF INCLUSION INITIATIVES – FREQUENCY & PRICE

Often seen

FREQUENCY

Rarely seen

- Women's Network
- Mentoring
- Anchoring the Equality Strategy in HR
- Leadership Programs for Women only
- Clear Communication
- Adjusting Recruitment Processes
- Unconcious Bias Training
- Workplace Flexibility
- Focus on Promotion Procedures and Career Planning
- Sponsoring
- Baseline Survey and Yearly Data Monitoring
- Educating Diversity Champions
- Synchronized Top Management
- Quotas
- Mandatory Leadership Training
- Mobilizing Men
- Anchoring D&I Strategy at the top

Low ——— PRICE ——— High

Figure 11.2 Matrix of inclusion initiatives: frequency and price

> *"Our goal is to have 50/50 male and female representation at all levels of the organisation, including executive leadership, by 2032."*
> *– Loren I. Shuster, Chief People Officer & Head of Corporate Affairs, The LEGO Group*

The 13 initiatives for accelerating gender balance in your organisation

Some of the 13 initiatives have been covered in much greater detail in earlier chapters, so please refer back to these for guidance on how to implement such initiatives. Here I will provide an overview and explain how they have a positive impact on creating gender balance.

#1 Baseline survey and annual data monitoring

> *"I am fact driven. Show me some stats and numbers on a fairly detailed level. That will force top management to open their eyes."*
> *– Male leader of leaders*

As we discovered in Chapter 6, all diversity intelligence initiatives need to be based on data from within your organisation, and the same goes for initiatives to improve gender balance. By identifying your organisation's challenges and gaps, the path to success will become much clearer.

It is a sad fact that even well-intentioned initiatives can have a negative effect on cultural transformation if they are the wrong initiatives. Often when we ask companies why they have taken a haphazard approach to gender balance and inclusion of diversity, and why they chose certain initiatives to advance the agenda, we receive answers such as: "It seemed easy and inexpensive," "They were the only actions we had heard about" and "We needed to do something immediately."

Introducing initiatives without understanding why there is an issue with gender balance in your business will set your cultural transformation back. Even if there is a burning desire to do *something* it is essential to slow down and carry out the baseline analysis first. What still amazes us is every time we analyse the results from the inclusion surveys, we see that the initiatives the company had introduced to create gender balance were in vain – they were a waste of time and money. Instead, once you have the results from your analysis, the initiatives with a provable positive impact can be put in place, and the pace of change will be significantly quicker. In other words, "You need to slow down to speed up."

#2 Synchronisation within top management

> "We all have our posh diversity policies. But sometimes it's just there because it has to be there – not because it's owned by top management."
>
> – Male leader of leaders

In Chapter 5, *Synchronising the Executive Team*, we explored this issue in detail. It has to come after you have collected your baseline data because you need top management to align around this and base their strategy, and therefore the initiatives they introduce, on what is happening within your organisation. This is about commitment and accountability and, again, it holds true across all D&I initiatives.

There are several questions that those in top management need to answer in relation to gender balance. They are: What is the untapped bottom-line potential of gender balance?[2] What is the risk of missing out on talent and failing to mirror the market/customers? What is the risk of having homogenous management teams when it comes to making increasingly complex decisions and navigating an unpredictable and diverse market?

In some cases, people further down the organisation will be looking for an excuse not to implement policies to improve gender balance. Any sign of doubt or hesitation among the people in top management will allow them to dismiss the initiatives being introduced. It is not possible to effect culture change if those in top management allow unacceptable patterns or behaviours that benefit one gender group over the other to persist.

#3 Top management taking responsibility for the equality strategy

"When I have seen it work, it worked because the top owned it. In large international corporations where I have worked, the message came from the top. They drew the big picture and pushed it."
– Male leader of leaders

Culture change surrounding gender balance will not happen if those in top management are not driving the agenda. In many cases, responsibility can be passed to the HR team and, even though they undoubtedly have an important role to play, they will not be able to create a culture change without top management leading the way.

HR departments often lack the resources to effectively implement policies to promote gender balance. When you have tried and failed multiple

---

[2]Credit Suisse (2019), *Gender Diversity Is Good for Business*.

times, as many organisations have, fatigue sets in and this makes it even more challenging to introduce new initiatives.

Board members are increasingly interested in leveraging the benefits associated with gender balance. However, they have to understand that they have to take responsibility for developing and guiding the gender balance strategy. There is significant evidence to show that putting responsibility in HR departments does not work when it comes to improving gender balance, so you have to ask why your company is persisting down a path that is likely doomed to fail.

#4 Educating D&I Champions

> *"I think for me one of the things I have picked up is that there are remarks (females and racial) being made behind closed doors, which is not okay. I hear it because I'm white and male, but I'm not comfortable with it. I notice as I'm a minority, despite my looks."*
> *– Male respondent to an inclusion survey*

In Chapter 8, we looked at the positive impact D&I Champions can have and looked in detail at how you can train them and who you can choose to perform this essential supporting role.

The key with D&I Champions is that they are acting on a clear mandate from top management, tying this initiative in with several of the others I have explored in this chapter, and which we have already covered in this book. Your D&I Champions need to have the authority, confidence, knowledge and skills to challenge the old culture and act as valuable partners in all the processes that need to change.

#5 Mobilising men

> "Women on maternity leave should have a raise equivalent to the men's. Make it visible."
>
> – Male leader of leaders

Mobilising men is one of the most powerful strategies for improving gender balance and yet it is the one that companies most frequently overlook. Among the organisations we work with at the Living Institute, who are introducing many positive initiatives and making progress on gender balance, barely any mobilise men. However, as men are the group who typically own and influence the culture in established organisations, engaging them in this agenda would speed up the process tremendously.

Often, however, gender balance initiatives become women-only projects. They mistakenly focus on "fixing" the women in an organisation, despite the fact that they do not need to be "fixed." This means these initiatives are not only ineffective at addressing gender balance, but are also insulting to female employees and can even result in more women leaving a company, rather than less.

Imagine how much stronger the case would be for gender balance if it came from men as well as women. Men are not at fault; in many cases they are simply unaware of the barriers and biases their female colleagues face on a daily basis. By making them aware and making them part of the gender balance conversation, you can send a powerful message and show that men are as much a part of the solution as women.

"I had no idea before how many privileges I had as a man. I lived in a bubble."

– From an interview with Caroline Farberger, CEO at ICA Försäkring AB, after gender reassignment surgery[3]

There is a desire among men to do more in this area and organisations can benefit greatly by tapping into that. Research has shown that four out of five men feel bad about the gender imbalance at their organisation and are looking for ways to change this element of the culture.[4]

Without mobilising men in your organisation to support and drive the gender balance agenda, you will not succeed in changing the culture. There is also research showing that, without male engagement, stereotypes about women will continue to thrive and spread.[5]

---

[3]Mosbech, H. (2020), "'Jeg anede ikke, hvor mange privilegier jeg havde.' Da topchefen skiftede køn og opdagede, at alt, hun troede om ligestilling, var forkert" ("'I had no idea how many privileges I had.' When the CEO changed gender and discovered that everything she thought about equality was wrong"), *Zetland*, 5 September 2020, available at: https://www.zetland.dk/historie/sejvJjNX-moBPQmW4-b2215.

[4]Global Institute for Women's Leadership at King's College London (2019), *International Women's Day 2019: Global Attitudes Towards Gender Equality*, available at: https://www.kcl.ac.uk/news/global-study-reveals-what-world-thinks-about-womens-equality.

[5]Flood, M., Russell, G., O'Leary, J., and Brown, C. (2017), *Men Make a Difference: How to Engage Men on Gender Equality, Synopsis Report*, Sydney, Diversity Council Australia.

Top tips for mobilising men

- Run facilitated workshops where men and women share common experiences relating to the benefits and barriers associated with gender balance.
- Run men-only "Barbershop" sessions, where men in groups of 10 meet regularly and share their stories, coach each other and commit to making a difference.

#6 Unconscious bias training

"It has taken me a while not to talk negatively about having kids. Now I have accepted it and I own being a mother AND a career woman. You must fight for being true to yourself on your way up the career ladder."
– Female with no management responsibilities

As we learned in Chapter 9, we all have unconscious biases. In fact, unconscious bias is one of the biggest barriers to diversity, inclusion and gender balance. It frequently leads to poor decision-making and missed opportunities. Where gender balance is concerned, it can often lead to women being overlooked for promotions and hinder their progression in an organisation.

Reducing unconscious bias within your organisation is important, but taken alone this initiative will have minimal impact. The fundamental culture of the organisation also needs to change, along with its structure and processes, for the benefits of unconscious bias training to be realised.

#7 Mandatory inclusive leadership training

> "In no way is it taken into consideration that women are different from men. They should be led and developed differently."
>   – Female without management responsibilities

This is a topic we explored in detail in Chapter 7. When it comes to creating gender balance, managers have to become the role models and frontrunners for an inclusive corporate culture. Inclusive leadership training can easily be fitted into existing leadership programmes and can include modules on unconscious bias, gender equality, age, cultural background, ethnicity, sexual orientation, religion and cultural intelligence.

Why mandatory? Because if this is only voluntary it implies that it is not a priority for top management.

#8 Adjusting recruitment processes

> "Women have to be 10% better than their male colleagues to get the same job."
>   – Female respondent to an inclusion survey

The HR team are important partners for those in management and have a vital role to play when it comes to creating gender balance within an organisation. It is essential to optimise recruitment processes to promote gender balance and minimise the structural barriers and biases throughout an organisation.

This ties in with initiatives relating to unconscious bias training, which is particularly important when it comes to recruitment as well as performance reviews, career planning and selecting candidates for talent and high-potential programmes.

Failing to make the necessary adjustments to your HR processes will simply mean that the outdated mechanisms in your old structure counteract any good work you are doing on improving gender balance.

Top tips for adjusting recruitment processes

- Management and key HR personnel to regularly review all critical processes influencing gender balance in management.
- Inform recruitment agencies about the business-critical nature of your gender balance goals to ensure you are presented with qualified male and female candidates for all vacancies.
- Select someone who is not involved in candidate selection to anonymise CVs before they go before the recruitment panel. There are also technical solutions that can do this. By removing candidates' names, photos and so on, you will present neutral CVs to those making recruitment decisions and remove the likelihood of unconscious bias clouding decision-making.
- Get applicants who pass the first selection round to complete a competency test to ensure that the final group of candidates is chosen based on competence alone. Only then do you consider whether the person you want to hire contributes to gender balance and diversity.

#9 Placing a focus on promotion procedures and career planning

"We could be bold and set new big goals to make sure that women are in the race. For example, by having at least ⅓ female candidates. If you don't have clear goals, nothing happens. It is self-evident: women are afraid of being alone as they advance, and they will be [without action]."

– Male leader of leaders

Career development supporting gender balance has to be systematic and include differences in gender-related behaviour. This is a topic that repeatedly comes up in the inclusion surveys we conduct with organisations around the world.

Some of the specific issues we regularly hear about include:

- A narrow focus on professional issues, rather than looking at the potential of the whole person and his/her contribution to the culture.
- Men tend to be more visible and more specific when advertising their ambitions.
- Women tend to be humbler than men and often it feels unnatural for them to overtly advertise their leadership competencies and ambitions.
- Women are seen as less ambitious when they choose not to act like men.
- Women are typically motivated by making a difference and working towards a common purpose and ambitions, but are frequently presented with different motivating factors.

Until your organisation develops a truly gender-balanced and inclusive culture, it is important to understand that women will need to be specifically encouraged and motivated, and that the approach taken with women will often need to be different to that taken with men.

Top tips for focusing on promotion procedures and career planning

- Measure managers on whether they support their employees' career development, qualifications and ambitions all year round, not only during the annual development meeting.
- Provide training to your teams so that they understand how men and women communicate differently. In particular, making male managers

> aware of this is essential to enable these honest and open conversations that are free from bias.
> - Encourage women to voice their leadership ambitions in a clear and confident way.

#10 Sponsorship

Running a sponsorship scheme for women with high potential can help them to reach the upper levels of management in an organisation more quickly. The key to an effective sponsorship programme is encouraging sponsors to actively support the women's career development through activities such as coaching and providing opportunities for networking.

As Hermina Ibarra argues in an article,[6] sponsorship differs from mentorship in that the sponsor is held accountable for the results that their sponsee achieves. One particularly effective way to achieve this is to set KPIs around sponsorship and to tie the success of a sponsor to their bonus payment. In short: a sponsor is a person who has power and will use it for you.

#11 Quotas

> *"We simply haven't moved the needle. That's why I feel this way. We have to have quotas."*
>
> *– Female leader of leaders*

---

[6]Ibarra, H. (2019), "A Lack of Sponsorship is Keeping Women from Advancing into Leadership", *Harvard Business Review*, 19 August 2019, available at: https://hbr.org/2019/08/a-lack-of-sponsorship-is-keeping-women-from-advancing-into-leadership.

There can often be resistance to introducing quotas, with women in particular often concerned about being hired because of their gender. However, quotas are an effective tool for driving up numbers that have been stalling for years.

When they are implemented correctly, quotas can have a number of positive benefits, including:

- Seeing more qualified women applying for management positions.
- Solving the gender balance pipeline problem.
- Allowing for the objective measurement of progress both within a company and on individual managerial levels.

The fact is that quotas are an effective solution to tackle this element of a company's culture quickly.[7] Setting quotas also sends a clear message that gender balance is an essential part of your recruitment process. By making quotas binding, you can also protect top management from its own biases.

Top tip for introducing quotas

We recommend a soft gender quota of 40/20/40, which means having a minimum representation of 40% of each gender, with 20% left open to allow your organisation to hire the people with the right competencies and talent for different roles.

---

[7]Christensen, J.F., and Muhr, S.L. (2019), "H(a)unting Quotas: An Empirical Analysis of the Uncanniness of Gender Quotas", *Ephemera: Theory & Politics in Organization*, Vol. 19: 77–105.

> This means you could have a 60/40 split of men to women, or vice versa, or a balance that is closer to 50/50. It improves gender balance while still giving you the freedom to recruit the best talent to your organisation, regardless of their gender.
>
> Initially, you may temporarily prefer candidates from the underrepresented gender, competencies being equal, to help move towards a critical mass for gender balance.

#12 Clear communication about culture change success

> *"Change communication and make it more appealing to women. Change career paths so they fit into women's life circumstances. As things are now, it is created by men, for men."*
> *– Female without management responsibilities*

Communicating both internally and externally about the success you are having with your culture change efforts can boost morale, maintain commitment and contribute to an environment that is healthier overall.

Clear communication is useful to bust myths and break down stereotypes. Equally importantly, this kind of clear communication helps actions and new language become part of your organisation's normal cultural behaviour. I shared some tips around communication in Chapter 4 that you can use here.

One of the best pieces of content to share is a video of the CEO explaining why and how the organisation is working towards gender balance.

#13 Workplace flexibility

> *"Someone said that she had experienced much more acceptance and understanding of women's family obligations. It is done in a totally different way."*
>
> *– Female leader of leaders*

All employees, regardless of their gender, need flexibility in their work environment sometimes. Men and women between the ages of 30 and 39 are known to find it particularly challenging to balance their work/career with their families.

Transparency is key when it comes to providing workplace flexibility, as is acknowledging that this benefits men and women alike. Creating a more flexible working environment is an effective way to prevent the long-term drain of talent in your organisation, both male and female.

A lack of flexibility is one of the main reasons why many qualified and ambitious women have been kept out of positions within top management. This is not because family life is more important to women than men, but because decision-makers consider family life to be a barrier to female ambition.

Top tips for introducing flexible working

There are several formal initiatives you can introduce to promote greater flexibility at work and benefit all your employees. They include:

- Ending late, and often unnecessarily long, afternoon meetings.
- Giving all employees the option to leave work early to pick up their kids and catch up at home later.
- Providing job share options to ease the workload and keep talent at your organisation during tough times.

The traps: gender balance initiatives to avoid

As I said at the beginning of this chapter, there are four initiatives that typically have no positive effect or, in many cases, a negative effect on your organisation's progress towards creating gender balance. Unfortunately, these are often also the initiatives that have already been introduced or attempted at many organisations.

I am going to briefly explain why these particular initiatives can be so damaging to your gender balance goals.

#1 Women's networks

There is no research that suggests that women-only networks positively impact the number of women in top management, or that they have a positive effect on female talent retention. In fact, in many cases the women in these networks simply confirm their bad experiences and sense of hopelessness in the lack of progress around gender balance. As a result, they often leave more quickly for roles in more progressive organisations where their experience, competencies and ambition are put to good use.

This initiative also implies that women are the ones with the problem and that they need to "fix" it on their own. This is counterproductive and, as we know by now, achieving gender balance is something that everyone in an organisation has to work towards.

Although such networks are often established with good intentions, they do little to contribute to the overall aim of solving gender balance problems.

#2 Placing responsibility for the equality strategy with HR

Your HR department has an essential role to play in terms of achieving cultural transformation. While it might be tempting and easy to place responsibility for the equality strategy in this department, it is almost always a mistake.

As I explained in Chapter 4, any successful gender balance or diversity strategy has to come from top management down. Due to its business-critical nature, responsibility for driving the equality strategy has to fall on those in top management, with HR in an important supporting role.

When HR departments are given responsibility for equality strategies, they almost invariably fail at creating the required culture change. The CEO, board and executive team need to be vocal in their support and express this support frequently. Another issue with this approach is that many managers or employees who are given the responsibility of implementing an equality agenda are stigmatised as feminists. This stigma is more frequently attached to female employees who are trying to push this agenda forward.[8]

#3 Mentoring

Mentoring and sponsorship might sound similar, but there is one crucial difference between such initiatives: responsibility. In a traditional mentoring programme, there is a lack of responsibility on the mentor if the mentee

---

[8]Johnson, S.K., and Hekman, D. (2016), "Women and Minorities Are Penalized for Promoting Diversity", *Harvard Business Review*, 23 March 2016, available at: https://hbr.org/2016/03/women-and-minorities-are-penalized-for-promoting-diversity.

does not progress. Mentoring typically involves informal meetings and no targets are set.

As a result, mentoring initiatives frequently fail to produce any meaningful results, and it is very rare for a mentee to reach a higher level in an organisation than her mentor.

#4 Women-only leadership programmes

Much like women's networks, this kind of initiative implies that it is women who have the problem. Many such programmes are designed to change women's behaviour (often to be more like men's) and, in doing so, the organisation loses the very benefits they are trying to realise by increasing gender balance and diversity.

These schemes also imply that, despite women's professionalism and ambitions, they lack something. For many women, this is insulting.

If you apply this thinking to another aspect of diversity, you can suddenly see how absurd this approach is. For example, would you ever think, "We are aware that it's tough to be a black person in certain contexts, so let's send them on a training course to become more white"? Of course, you would never do this! It is offensive and it does not work. Women-only leadership initiatives are no different.

Employees are, in fact, demanding the opposite of what these training programmes deliver: diverse and authentic leadership styles that are appreciated within the company's culture.

> *"Inclusion ensures that you actually use all the competence found in the room. You take advantage of the entire management."*
> *– From an interview with Caroline Farberger, CEO at ICA Försäkring AB, after gender reassignment surgery*[9]

Summary

Creating gender balance does not have to be hard and, in fact, many of the most effective initiatives are easier and more cost-effective to implement than you may imagine. It is important that, whatever initiatives you include in your strategy, they are based on data. You cannot tackle this problem blind.

Mobilising men is one of the most important aspects to focus on, because only when everyone is working towards gender balance can real cultural transformation take place.

Pushing forward the gender balance agenda is not a blame game, but must be seen as a necessity to enable organisations to survive in, and navigate, this VUCA world in which we are now living and working.

---

[9]Mosbech, H. (2020), "'Jeg anede ikke, hvor mange privilegier jeg havde.' Da topchefen skiftede køn og opdagede, at alt, hun troede om ligestilling, var forkert" ("'I had no idea how many privileges I had.' When the CEO changed gender and discovered that everything she thought about equality was wrong"), *Zetland*, 5 September 2020, available at: https://www.zetland.dk/historie/sejvJjNX-moBPQmW4-b2215.

Part 3

Models/Recommendations for Change

So far I have explained why it is imperative to focus on diversity and inclusion within your organisation. It is not an exaggeration to say that if you are unable to make progress in this area, your business may cease to exist in the future.

In Part 2, I explored what specific areas you have to focus on to introduce successful D&I strategies and how you can drive cultural transformation within your organisation. As well as exploring the essential role of top management in any D&I agenda, I also delved into some of the most effective strategies you can use to roll out an impactful D&I strategy that leads to genuine and lasting cultural change.

I also specifically examined gender balance, which is a different issue to diversity. Although some of the initiatives you can use to create gender balance are the same as those for increasing diversity, there are others, such as mobilising men, that are specific to gender balance.

Understanding the traps that many organisations fall into when they are working towards gender balance is also useful, as it can help you avoid implementing initiatives that are doomed to fail and instead focus on what really works.

In this final part of the book, I am going to share some resources you can use to assist with cultural transformation at your organisation as you move towards creating a diverse and inclusive working environment. I will also offer recommendations for change and examine what the future holds for D&I.

Chapter 12

Resources: The Four Steps Towards Inclusivity

We are going to return to the wheel that I shared with you at the beginning of Part 2, because this tendency to jump straight to action (Step 4) really is the smoking gun in terms of why so many D&I initiatives have repeatedly failed at organisations all over the world.

As you have learned, there are three steps that we need to take first:

1. Drive: understanding why D&I is important to your organisation and how failing to take action will affect your company.
2. Knowledge: what is really happening in your organisation? What do the numbers and results of an inclusion survey show? What are your employees, managers and customers saying about the current state of D&I in your organisation?
3. Strategy: work backwards from where you want to be in two or five years' time to find solutions that will actually work. Identify who needs to be involved and what elements of the culture you need to change. Decide what initiatives need to be introduced, when and who needs to be a part of them.

We're going to build a factory. . .

David is the CEO of a manufacturing firm. One day, his COO Alan comes to talk to him and says, "I just wanted to let you know, we're going to build a factory in China."

David is a little blindsided, "Okay, why are we going to build a factory in China? We haven't spoken about this in any detail at all."

Alan replies, "At the last board meeting you mentioned that you wanted us to expand into Asian markets, so we're going to build a factory in China. A lot of other businesses are doing the same."

David is almost lost for words. "Hang on a minute. I said we should explore moving into Asian markets, not just jump straight in without looking first. Why China? What's the factory going to produce? How much is this all going to cost? What are the returns we're expecting? Is this even the right way to break into Asian markets?" David's head is swimming with all the unanswered questions.

"We have to be more strategic about this. China might not even be the best place to start. Just because our competitors are going in that direction, it doesn't mean we should just follow them. We have no data to back up our decision-making," David continues.

"We are not going to just build a factory in China. Can't you hear how ridiculous that sounds?"

Alan takes all of this in. It is as though a fog lifts. "Of course you're right. Sorry, I just got carried away and jumped straight into action. We'll do this properly."

Could you ever imagine a situation in business where you would make a decision in the same way that Alan did, with so little data to support it and so little strategy surrounding it? You might even be thinking that if Alan was your COO you would fire him on the spot!

The problem is many businesses do exactly what Alan did when they make decisions about how to tackle issues with gender balance, diversity and inclusion. They jump straight to action and choose an initiative without any of the necessary research, data or strategy to support that decision or make it a success. This is why so many businesses go round in circles with their D&I initiatives, never seeming to make any progress despite the best of intentions.

THE WHEEL OF CULTURAL TRANSFORMATION

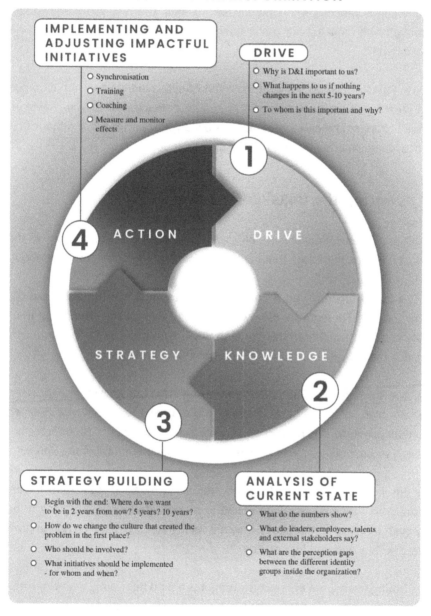

Figure 12.1 The wheel of cultural transformation

Only once you have completed Steps 1 to 3 do you arrive at Step 4: Action. This process will hopefully feel familiar. It is the same one you go through when making any major business decision and D&I initiatives are no different.

In Part 2, I shared some of the most effective initiatives when it comes to creating diversity, inclusion and gender balance, but in your haste to make changes, be careful not to rush blindly into any of them without first uncovering what is required at *your* organisation.

Answering the unasked questions

I will use unconscious bias training as an example, because it is one of the most common initiatives that companies contact the Living Institute about.

In fact, I recently had a conversation with an IT startup about exactly this training. The conversation was a familiar one for me. The Living Institute received a call from this company looking to book us to deliver unconscious bias training as part of their onboarding process.

The IT company in question is relatively new, but growing rapidly. They have a high level of cultural diversity and are keen to attract more women to their company. The person who contacted us was not the HR director, but was a young man who was a member of the company's Diversity Council.

His intentions were well placed, but, sadly, offering 30-minute unconscious bias training sessions online to all new starters is not going to be enough to improve the issues they are facing around inclusion and improving diversity and gender balance.

During the course of our conversation, I asked this young man why inclusion of diversity is important at his organisation, whether top management is aligned with the strategy, who does and does not feel included at the organisation and whether they planned to provide any training for existing members of staff, not just those who are new to the company.

He did not have the answers to these questions. This is in no way his fault. It is a situation I have seen time and time again, and the perception that unconscious bias training is some kind of magic pill that will "fix" problems with diversity and inclusion persists in many organisations all over the world.

As I am sure you are now aware, I can tell you from experience that there is no magic pill for creating diversity and inclusion in your organisation, and unconscious bias training certainly is not the silver bullet that many businesses seem to hope for.

Taking three steps back

In my conversation with this young man from the IT startup, I explained that we needed to take a few steps back before we started offering unconscious bias training. Look at the wheel that I shared earlier in the chapter. You can see the questions we need to answer and the steps we need to take.

Understanding why D&I is important to the organisation and ensuring that this understanding starts in top management and filters all the way down is the first step. Before you make any decisions about what to do next, carrying out a gap analysis to identify the specific issues your organisation is facing is essential. This data collection is Step 2.

In fact, in carrying out this gap analysis, Step 3 becomes much easier, because it often provides you with a clear roadmap of what you need to do to improve things. The key, as with any good strategy, is in starting from a place of knowledge and understanding what is happening and where the issues truly lie.

During my conversation with the man from the IT company, he told me that there is a "them-and-us" culture developing among employees from the same cultural backgrounds and that there had been some jokes and stereotyping happening. When he started the conversation with me, he believed that providing unconscious bias training would eliminate unconscious bias within the organisation and create a culture of inclusion.

However, as I informed him, there is no magic pill when it comes to creating a culture of inclusion, and even with the best unconscious bias training in the world, it is not possible to eliminate unconscious bias from an organisation.

Why the focus on unconscious bias training?

There is no doubt that unconscious bias is one of the biggest barriers to inclusion and diversity. Businesses are aware of the role it plays and know that it is an area they cannot afford to ignore. However, as with our IT startup, many jump straight to offering training without first understanding where the unconscious biases within their organisation lie.

My conversation with the IT startup was similar to conversations I have had with many other businesses, and I am sure that I will continue to have. Unconscious bias training, when run correctly, is certainly valuable. However, it has to be part of a broader D&I strategy that seeks to solve the issues specific to your company, and it has to run in parallel with other initiatives.

The framework I have shared here will not only mean that your unconscious bias training is more effective, but also that it works as part of a whole package of initiatives designed to create lasting cultural transformation.

You might be surprised by what you find

When you carry out the gap analysis and inclusion surveys in Step 2, you might be surprised by what you uncover. At the Living Institute, we are less and less surprised by what we see, but for many companies the data we present to them comes as a shock.

For an organisation like the IT startup, it could also be beneficial to survey customers. That particular company sells its services to the public sector in Denmark, where there are more female decision-makers. It could be useful for them to learn how their customers feel about always dealing with non-Danish-speaking men within the IT sector, for instance.

Often, seeing the results of this baseline analysis opens people's eyes to issues they were previously blind to. All of a sudden they can see the signs everywhere. In some cases, they discover that the problems lie somewhere other than where they thought. In others, they discover there are more issues to deal with than they initially realised.

Suddenly becoming aware of issues can make you feel as though you need to rush to tackle them. However, it is important that you do not skip Step 3. Without a strategy, even the right initiatives will have minimal impact.

Set goals alongside your strategy

When you build your strategy, it is important that you also set goals that you can measure your progress against. When do you want to see gender balance in your organisation? How will you be able to tell when certain cultural issues are no longer in play?

Having these goals allows you to effectively measure the progress of any initiatives you introduce in Step 4. Your goals can also help you to reverse engineer your strategy, by allowing you to examine what has caused a particular issue within your organisation's culture and who needs to be involved in order for the initiatives going forward to have the greatest positive impact on diversity and inclusion in your workplace.

It is only once you have completed Steps 1 to 3 that you can then talk about what specific initiatives will make you stronger and help you solve the issues you have identified in your company. It is at this point that you can reach out for assistance with running unconscious bias training or another initiative.

The wheel keeps turning

The reason our diagram is a wheel rather than a straight line is that it keeps spinning. Once you take action, you come back to Step 1 and your drive. After implementing an initiative, you have to measure and monitor the results. This will allow you to adjust your strategy accordingly and maybe take a different action in one or two years' time.

You work around that wheel time and time again, always examining your why, collecting the data you need to support your decision-making, using that data to create and then adjust your strategy and, finally, implementing initiatives and evolving them as time goes on.

Succeeding with your D&I strategy involves taking a targeted approach that is based on data, rather than throwing initiatives out there and hoping that one of them works.

Summary

Following these four steps, in the right order, is one of the biggest factors in the success of D&I initiatives. Businesses that go straight to Step 4 and bypass the first three steps often end up implementing initiatives that are not only ineffective but also counterproductive.

However, in my experience, many businesses rush straight to Step 4 because they are desperate to do *something*. Taking the time to complete Steps 1 to 3 will pay dividends though, because it will ensure that when you do reach Step 4 and take action, the actions you take are the ones that will have a positive impact on your company's culture and the levels of inclusion. Although it initially might seem to take longer, it will significantly speed up your progress in the long run.

This is a process that has to be repeated, ensuring that initiatives are evaluated and adjusted accordingly to bring about the desired cultural change in your organisation.

Chapter 13

The Future of D&I in the Workplace

So far I have talked a lot about what is happening now, as well as what you can do within your organisation to create a cultural transformation and improve D&I – but what does the future hold? There are several areas that I believe will be important in the future of D&I, starting with finances.

Show me the money

The financial impact of failing to improve D&I is clear. Look at the example I shared earlier in the book about Goldman Sachs, which will no longer list companies that do not include women in their top management.

This shows that the financial penalty for not taking action is already too big to continue as we have in the past. However, in terms of financial performance, the gap between businesses that embrace diversity, inclusion and gender balance and those that do not will only get wider.

This is already happening and the impact that a lack of diversity and inclusion has will only become more prominent as time passes.

Referring back to Robert Næss in Chapter 2, the Chief Investment Officer and Portfolio Manager at Nordea,[1] who recently said that, after looking at 40,000 companies worldwide, he estimates that companies with a female CEO or female board of directors outperform other companies by 21%. That is a huge difference. Based on those figures, it would be fair to estimate that in the future, we are likely to see more female CEOs than male CEOs.

This is not only a matter of which companies make more money, it is a matter of survival. Think about Kodak. The company did not manage to digitalise its products and, although it still exists, it is no longer considered a major player in the photography market like it once was. Many other businesses that did not keep up with the digital revolution suffered a similar fate or simply disappeared. In fact, if you look at the list of the largest companies in the world today, you will see that many of them did not exist 15 or 20 years ago.

Let us look at this from a different perspective. At the 2021 Abundance 360 Conference, which is an innovative technology event run by Peter Diamandis of the Singularity University, they were talking about flying cars and the models that are *already* in production. In fact, flying cars are expected to be a normal part of life by 2030. Can you imagine that we will have developed flying cars and yet there could still be companies trying to exclude women from top management? It does not make sense that we would have progressed so far in one way and be so behind in another.

---

[1]Nordea (2017), "Investing in Female CEOs Pays Off", available at: https://www.nordea.com/en/press-and-news/news-and-press-releases/news-en/2017/investing-in-female-ceos-pays-off.html.

A matter of survival

Diversity and inclusion is becoming increasingly business critical: 10 out of 10 CEOs that we speak to at the Living Institute describe it as a business-critical issue. They know that if they do not find a way to improve diversity and create an inclusive culture, their business will cease to exist.

We are at a crucial turning point at the time of writing this book. We still have one foot in the past, a world where we have to cope with all the negative aspects of exclusion, such as harassment and discrimination. Although we are still used to this negativity in many workplaces, our tolerance for it is changing.

The boomer generation can cope with that negativity, but younger generations cannot and, more accurately, do not want to. As a result, they are more conscious about where they want to work and actively seek out organisations that have values they can buy into. They want to have a purpose in their work life, which means companies that do not have a strong purpose and focus on sustainability will have to face the consequences of younger generations turning their backs on them.

All of this adds up to even bigger financial downsides to failing to address issues surrounding diversity and inclusion in the future. CEOs know this is the case, but many of them are still struggling to make the necessary changes and transformations within their organisations.

To succeed with their D&I initiatives in the future, CEOs will need to take a deeper look at what went wrong with their past attempts to drive their D&I agenda forward. For some this will be more painful than others, especially if they have spent 20 or even 30 years working on D&I and failing to see an impact.

CEOs will increasingly be measured by how they manage D&I within their organisations, and those who fail to master D&I will be punished.

All of this means that businesses no longer have a choice about whether to embrace D&I and push for change on this agenda. Getting D&I right is essential for the survival of businesses.

It is a simple fact of nature that companies that have a worse financial performance than their competitors die, and strong financial performance is becoming much more closely tied to success within D&I.

D&I initiatives will gather pace

The CEOs and other members of top management who do succeed in mastering D&I at their organisations will find themselves increasingly in the spotlight. They will become the superstars of this agenda and other companies will look to them to find out what they have to do to follow in their footsteps.

As a result, the businesses that have been lagging behind will start to mimic the ones that have succeeded. This will eventually mean that all the initiatives that do not work, or that are counterproductive to advancing the D&I agenda, will simply stop being options that companies turn to.

Instead, businesses will introduce the initiatives and actions that they have seen are successful in other organisations, leading to genuine change. I am already starting to see a movement in this direction through my work in D&I.

The result of more businesses emulating the ones that are succeeding with D&I will be that the rate of change accelerates. Rather than seeing companies' D&I strategies stagnating for 20 or 30 years, we will see companies developing D&I strategies that work. The more companies that succeed, the more will follow in their footsteps. The more success stories there are, the quicker it will be for other businesses to implement similar strategies and the greater the pace of change in the D&I landscape.

Businesses that don't keep up will lose talent

As I said earlier, younger generations will refuse to work for businesses that do not align with their values and demonstrate high levels of diversity and inclusion. This will become more than just a recruitment challenge. It will also lead to highly talented individuals leaving companies. I even have anecdotal evidence that this is happening already.

In June 2020, I spoke to a British man who holds a high-level position within a multi-national energy company. At that time, he told me that, if nothing had changed around diversity and inclusion at his firm by the end of the year, he would leave and become a house husband. He told me this would allow his wife to "follow the brilliant career path that she's already on".

This multi-national company stands to lose a highly talented individual because they are not doing enough on D&I. As well as the obvious loss of his talent, there will be financial consequences to this person leaving his job.

Mindsets are changing

Becoming diverse and inclusive is a business imperative. Without making such a change, companies will not survive.

We can see how a similar scenario played out in the 1990s when companies adopted a value-driven strategy and leadership style, although where D&I is concerned, I believe it really will be "do or die" for businesses.

If you look at the businesses that succeeded in the 1990s, they were typically the organisations that succeeded in getting all their employees to live and work by their values. Those values were ingrained in every aspect of the business and they created a cultural transformation in doing so.

Businesses are on a similar journey now to what they faced in the 1990s. However, when it comes to D&I, it is even more urgent. Some businesses in the 1990s did not adopt this value-driven approach and still managed to survive. I do not think that will be the case now for companies that fail to make the necessary changes surrounding D&I.

There is no doubt that cultural transformations such as these are complex, but are they doable? Absolutely.

Mindsets among those in top management are changing and the executives who are unable to shift their mindsets to prioritise D&I will find themselves out of a job. I encountered one executive who told me that working towards gender balance was discrimination against men. If this is the attitude that gender balance or D&I initiatives are met with by your board, I am sorry to say they are leading your company towards failure.

Dark clouds on the horizon

However, these attitudes are among the dark clouds I see on the D&I horizon. There are many movements around the world that are trying to divide rather than unite and include.

There are sadly many examples where people appear to be moving backwards on diversity and inclusion. I recently read about a political movement in France that is ultra right-wing. Women are not welcome and neither are people of colour or those who are not French nationals. Then there are the likes of QAnon, which shares views that are poison to D&I agendas.

In order for not only businesses, but society as a whole, to move towards a more inclusive future, action must consciously be taken to stop this mindset spreading to more people. At the time of writing, we have these two movements: one pushing for greater inclusion and unity and the other calling for division and exclusion, and we have yet to see which will win.

There is also the danger that fatigue with seeing initiatives to improve diversity and inclusion failing, in both businesses and society, has set in for some and they are struggling to believe in a brighter future.

Although we are seeing great progress on D&I in some places, it would not be right to talk about the future of D&I without acknowledging these dark clouds and the growing resistance we are seeing in some quarters of society. This will naturally have an effect on D&I in business.

Inclusion will become universal

Despite the challenges we are facing in the present day, I believe that one day, inclusion will become a universal aspect of companies and an integral element of their culture. We are not likely to achieve this in the near future, but eventually there will be no alternative to inclusion, because any alternative will simply be unacceptable.

However, we cannot afford to be complacent. While there is certainly a change happening, that change is not inevitable. It takes effort and the conscious implementation of the right thinking, programmes and strategies to ensure inclusion is cemented, not only within our businesses but within society as a whole.

As I have already mentioned, people, particularly in younger generations, are becoming increasingly aware of and sensitive to discrimination, harassment and unfair treatment of others. As our collective mindset shifts further in this direction, conversations will become much more focused on inclusion and we will talk less about diversity.

This is already a change that I have noticed in my work with clients, where I hear more and more of them talking about fostering inclusion, because there is a growing awareness that diversity without inclusion is actually a terrible option.

Many companies have been trying to change their numbers for many years and have spent a huge amount of money on recruiting a more diverse workforce. However, if there is an exclusionary culture at a company, these employees will leave as quickly as you can hire new ones.

This is an issue frequently highlighted in our inclusion surveys and one that a growing number of companies are coming to acknowledge. When people feel excluded, they do not thrive, they are not happy and they cannot wait to leave that company as quickly as possible.

As businesses wake up to this issue, their priorities will increasingly shift towards making a cultural transformation to develop a culture of inclusion.

From D&I to I&N

Ultimately, this is not about the future of D&I in the workplace, but actually about the future of I&N in the workplace: inclusivity and normality.

Why would I want us to change the name from D&I to I&N? The reason is really very simple: as long as we talk about diversity, we continue to put people in boxes. If you have this colour skin, you belong over there. If you are of this gender, then you go here. If you are transgender, you are in this group. If you are from this cultural background, you slot in over there.

Although there is a lot to be said for diversity, often our conversations around the topic involve dividing people into different identity groups. One of my friends is a German, atheist, transgender lesbian born in Turkey. Which box does she belong in?

Eventually I expect to see the field of D&I shift away from talking about diversity to having conversations about humanity. Diversity will become normal. The norms that we have will allow us to be ourselves in many different ways.

Inclusion will still be the mantra that runs through this because, as we know, as soon as you have exclusion everything else falls apart.

What do you see in your future?

It can be very easy to get absorbed by the business arguments for diversity and inclusion and to forget about the wider positive impacts it has on the people in your life. Moving forward on the D&I agenda is not only about your business, it is about being able to look your seven-year-old granddaughter in the eye and tell her that the future is just as bright for her as it is for her brothers.

Many people at the top in business claim that their organisation has a greater impact than simply making money. If this is something you believe, but you are holding back on making meaningful changes in relation to diversity and inclusion, it is time to shift your thinking. Can you honestly say you are working towards a better future while upholding the repression of many groups within society?

These are not random people you do not know. They are your wives, sisters, daughters, grandchildren, neighbours. This goes beyond simply business. It is ethical, social and a matter of community.

What gives me hope for the future is that there are many people in positions of power within business who want to change the status quo. Not all of them know what they need to do to create this brighter future for everyone, but the desire to see a change is a vital first step.

Where will it end? Despite the challenges we face, I can only see one outcome. We are heading towards the light at the end of the tunnel and it is not a train that is coming towards us, but the sun that is breaking through the darkness.

Chapter 14

Where Do You Go
from Here?

Diversity is everywhere. Even when you have what looks like a homogenous group of people, you will soon discover that there are many differences between them if you take the time to look. Many of the perceived problems relating to diversity do not result from diversity itself, but from a lack of inclusion.

Inclusion is the key to any cultural transformation. One of the big barriers to inclusion is the concept of covering, which I explored in more detail in Chapter 9 about unconscious bias. It is not only people who are part of minority groups or women who cover in the workplace. The majority of us do it, men and women alike, across all cultural and ethnic backgrounds.

When we cover, we are trying to hide the parts of ourselves that are different to those we would normally compare ourselves with. Diversity is therefore everywhere, even if it is not immediately obvious. The cultural change we need to see is a celebration of this diversity. We need to become aware of how different we actually are and leverage those differences to build more innovative and effective companies and societies.

Once we understand that diversity is everywhere, creating an inclusive environment where we can be true to ourselves becomes the imperative. This is an environment where people do not feel they need to cover and where we are all in a position to bring our ideas, knowledge, thoughts and skills to the table.

Without inclusion, everybody suffers. A lack of inclusion in the workplace does not only negatively affect minorities, even though they may feel it most keenly. You can see this is true if you look at the conflicts that arise even in what appear to be homogenous environments. Why are there still conflicts if everybody is "the same"? This is because, in actual fact, we are all different.

Having diversity in your organisation is not a choice you make. It is already there. The key to unlocking the enormous potential diversity offers is inclusion.

Change is coming

It is almost as if there is a perfect storm in the diversity and inclusion landscape at the time of writing this book. Time is up for continuing to operate in the same way you always have. The vast majority of people, not only those who are part of minority groups, understand how important it is to move forward on diversity and inclusion.

The timing is perfect for seeing a positive shift in the D&I landscape, and these changes are happening for the right reasons. There is no need to continue making the mistakes of the past, because research and real-life experience has shown us what we need to do to make things happen and to make real progress with D&I. We are in a very different place to where we were even two years ago and the pace of change is accelerating.

Inclusion is a mindset

Creating an inclusive culture has to come from the top. Everyone in top management has to understand why D&I is crucial and they have to align behind achieving inclusion as a strategic goal.

When we have conducted inclusion surveys in organisations that are highly inclusive, we find that most people are unable to say what steps they took to make that organisation inclusive. It is almost as if it is simply coming out of the walls. However, when we dig a little deeper, we often discover that there is a shared mindset of inclusivity, running all the way from the CEO through the majority of the other employees and managers.

The key to creating this kind of inclusive environment, where everybody agrees that it is the best place to work, is in having the mechanisms in place to attract people who contribute to that culture and to make sure they feel heard, seen and nurtured.

By attracting talent wherever you find it and allowing that talent to blossom, and by repeating this over and over again, you will build a company that everyone loves working for and where everyone can honestly say they feel included.

Only fools rush in

If you have read this book and want to create a diverse and inclusive culture at your company, do not rush and do not repeat the mistakes others have made. There are countless examples of how *not* to create inclusion and there are so many ways to fail.

There might be far fewer ways to create an inclusive and diverse organisation than there are to create a culture of exclusion, but the methods and strategies I have shared with you in this book work. They are not rocket science. They simply require careful thought and a willingness to learn and change.

One of the most important things to do is pause and not jump straight into action. Assess, evaluate and learn. Open your eyes to what is really going on. Basing your decisions on how to proceed on data from within your organisation is one of the single most important things you can do, and one that will lead to great positive change.

Get the support you need

Although D&I might not be rocket science, that does not mean it is easy. We are talking about cultural transformation, often on a large scale, and although you might know that it is important to change, that does not mean there will not be some resistance.

Getting D&I right requires knowledge, competencies and skill. Seek out people with that knowledge, competency and skill to work closely with the CEO and others in top management to develop a strategy based on data and to introduce initiatives that will actually work.

You cannot pretend that issues surrounding diversity and inclusion do not exist. Employees share negative stories with each other and are very sensitive to what is happening in a company. This is not a problem to sweep under the carpet; it is one you have to own and work hard to solve.

This may mean you have to make difficult decisions, because there is no room for those who do not support this agenda. As the saying goes, it only takes one rotten apple to turn the whole thing sour. If one person in the executive team undermines what the organisation is trying to do in terms of D&I, they are undermining the business's ultimate strategic goal of surviving. There is no place for them in your company if you are serious about creating a culture of inclusion.

The good news is that there is plenty of support available for companies that want to change. External organisations, like the Living Institute, can help you equip your leaders and managers with the tools and skills they need to become inclusive leaders. In our experience, once you get your managers and leaders on board with the agenda and you provide them with the skills they need to make it work, cultural transformation follows.

When it comes to synchronising those in top management around this agenda, and we know that this is essential for a D&I strategy to succeed, it often requires outside help. Your executives and board members will need assistance from skilled management strategists to develop a strategy that will work.

You will probably need to use a different process to create a strategy that will embed inclusion in the DNA of your organisation, lead to wholesale cultural transformation and ensure your business's long-term survival. This is too important to get wrong.

As I have explained, your D&I strategy has to be based on data, and to gather that data, you need to conduct an inclusion survey. This is where the Living Institute can begin to provide support. We are available to assist with every step of your journey, from the inclusion survey through to synchronising top management, providing inclusive leadership training and helping all your employees develop the skills they need to create and thrive in an inclusive culture.

Our services encompass training, counselling, educating, measuring and monitoring. Use our knowledge, skills and experience to propel your business towards a brighter, more inclusive future.

Become the role model you want to see

As Geena Davis said, "If you can see it, you can be it."[1] There are companies that not only have inclusive cultures, but that are thriving *because* of their inclusive culture. You can see it is possible. As you transform your culture, you will become a role model, not only for other businesses but also for minority groups and people of all gender identities.

There are many upsides to becoming this role model. You will keep talented people at your organisation for many years and they will demonstrate loyalty to your business, not to mention the multitude of financial benefits associated with greater diversity and inclusion.

I hope that, if you could not already, you can now clearly see the strong case for diversity and inclusion in every workplace.

Diversity and inclusion do not come at the expense of business performance, in fact the opposite is true. Now that you are fully aware of how much diversity and inclusion can give you, think again about everything you stand to lose if you choose to stay on a path defined by homogeneity and exclusion.

You have reached a fork in the road. Will you choose the path that only leads in one direction, towards the past and business failure, or will you choose the path that leads to a brighter and more prosperous future for all? I very much hope you choose the latter.

---

[1]Geena Davis, Institute on Gender in Media, available at: https://seejane.org.

ABOUT THE AUTHOR

Heidi R. Andersen is one of Europe's leading experts and a thought leader on Inclusion & Diversity. She is an in-demand keynote speaker, diversity facilitator, lecturer, media contributor and the mother of two daughters. As a serial entrepreneur, she founded the consultancy and centre of applied diversity intelligence, the Living Institute, in 2004.

She is passionate about the growth aspects of enhancing diversity, inclusivity and gender equity – both on a company level and an individual level. Teams of social scientists have tirelessly hunted for and found the answers to the questions many organisations keep asking: Why has it not happened yet? What is taking so long? What works – fast?

Based on studies, research and 17 years of experience, she and her team have found the magic pill to create sustainable results: applied diversity intelligence.

In her capacity as Applied Diversity Intelligence Facilitator, Heidi has worked with renowned companies such as Engie, Deloitte, LEGO®, Carlsberg, Esprit, SAP, L'Oréal, Bayer and many more, to introduce impactful initiatives to enhance inclusivity, diversity and gender balance.

Having worked with senior executives and at practically all levels in organisations, Heidi is familiar with what it takes to fast-forward the journey towards a truly inclusive company capable of attracting and retaining the best employees and talents no matter what they look like.

She has worked in the US, UK, India, Germany, Norway, Sweden, Iceland, Slovenia, Estonia, Norway and Portugal.

Heidi studied Strategy, Growth and Great Change Leadership Strategies on Innovation at Wharton Business School, University of Pennsylvania, US, and she is a certified LEGO® Serious Play® Practitioner.

If you would like to learn more about our work at the Living Institute, or find out how we can help your organisation, please contact: Heidi R. Andersen, info@livinginstitute.com, LIVING INSTITUTE, +45 35262626.

INDEX